VISITOR'S GUIDE TO ARANJUEZ

THE ROYAL SEAT OF ARANJUEZ

by José Luis Sancho

© EDITORIAL PATRIMONIO NACIONAL. 1996
   Palacio Real de Madrid
   Bailén, s/n
   28071 MADRID
   Tel. 547.53.50
© ALDEASA. 1996
© Of the texts: José Luis Sancho Gaspar

N.I.P.O. 006-98-005-6

Depósito Legal: M-24477-1997
I.S.B.N. 84-7120-224-7
I.S.B.N. 84-8003-078-X

Design and layout: Alberto Caffaratto
Photographs: Patrimonio Nacional, Félix Lorrio
Translation: Mervyn Samuel

Photomechanics: Lucam

Cover illustration: Palace of Aranjuez by Francesco Battaglioli

Printed by: Estudios Gráficos Europeos S. A., Madrid

Impreso en España, *Printed in Spain.*

April 1998

INDEX

PRESENTATION 5

INTRODUCTION 7
The Royal Residence for Springtime. 7
Nature subjected to control during the
reign of Philip II: tree-lined avenues,
orchards and gardens. 8
The Bourbons: Royal Aranjuez, model of
a court town and of a major agricultural
undertaking. 9
The nineteenth and twentieth centuries. 11

ARRIVAL IN ROYAL ARANJUEZ 12
Plaza de San Antonio. 13

**THE ROYAL PALACE AND
ITS GARDENS** 14
THE ROYAL PALACE 15

THE KING'S GARDEN AND THE PALACE PARTERRE 34
THE ISLAND GARDEN 37

**THE PRINCE'S GARDEN, THE ROYAL
BARGE MUSEUM AND THE
REAL CASA DEL LABRADOR** 45
THE PRINCE'S GARDEN 45
THE REAL CASA DEL LABRADOR 51

URBAN LAYOUT OF ARANJUEZ 65

BIBLIOGRAPHY 66

MAPS INSIDE THE COVERT

PRESENTATION

National Heritage is the institution which manages those properties of the State which are at the service of the Crown for performing representative functions as commended by the Constitution and Laws of Spain.

The institution manages a number of Palaces, as well as several Monasteries and Convents founded by Spanish monarchs, all of great historical, artistic and cultural importance and, most significantly, of great *symbolic value*. The Royal Palaces of Madrid, El Pardo, Aranjuez, San Ildefonso and La Almudaina are used as residential and representative buildings as was intended when they were built centuries ago and it is here where His Majesty the King performs his duties as Head of State, particularly in the Royal Palace of Madrid, where this *symbolic value* is felt most strongly, as the official residence of the Crown.

In harmony with these functions, the other buildings and properties which make up National Heritage have a decidedly cultural purpose and are places of study and research, as well as being open to the general public.

Both the buildings and the Spanish royal collections (27 in all, ranging from fans to tools and which include silverware, paintings, tapestries, furniture, musical instruments, watches, etc.) are remarkable for a number of characteristics which go to make National Heritage a unique cultural institution: their *particular purpose*, as they are still considered valid for representative use by the Crown; their *historical authenticity*, as they are all pieces which have been ordered, acquired or offered as gifts at some time for that particular place; their *originality*, which can be seen by the absence of replicas and imitations, and their *extraordinary artistic, historical and symbolic value*.

The combination of such impressive characteristics makes it clear to the visitor that National Heritage is much more than a simple museum.

The Spanish Royal Palaces are surrounded by approximately 20,500 hectares of open land. Around 500 hectares are given over to gardens or farmland, while the remaining 20,000 hectares are forest, divided between El Pardo, La Herrería and Riofrío and part of which is open to the general public. These woodlands, mainly of the biotype *Mediterranean forest*, are of renowned ecological importance, the value of which is at a par with the monuments found in their midst.

The Royal Monasteries and Convents have been attended by the same religious orders since their foundation, with the exception of San Lorenzo de El Escorial, originally of the Hieronymite Order, which was passed over to the Augustinian Order following the sale of Church lands in the 19th century. They enjoy particular importance in the history of Spain, as their origin dates back to the particular patronage of the monarchs of the era.

By being open to the general public, not only do these buildings fulfil a cultural purpose, they allow the Spanish people to capture their symbolic value, identify with it and consider themselves a legatee of the vast historical and artistic treasures which make up the properties of National Heritage.

Collected over the centuries by the Crown, their influence in the cultural identity of Spain has been, and still is, decisive.

INTRODUCTION

The fertile lands surrounding Aranjuez, located in the extensive vale where the River Jarama flows into the Tagus, are a virtual oasis set amidst the dry plains lying to the south of Madrid. When the Taifa Kingdom of Toledo was conquered by Alfonso VI of Castile at the end of the eleventh century, the Christian King transferred these privileged lands to the Military Order of Santiago in recompense for its important participation in battle. The Grand Masters of Santiago possessed a pleasure palace situated on the same site as the present one, and during the thirteenth, fourteenth and fifteenth centuries they improved the productivity of the land, cultivated mostly by Mudejars (Arabs living under Christian rule).

During Queen Isabel's reign at the end of the fifteenth century, the post of Grand Master of the Order was assimilated to the Crown; as a result, the lands of Aranjuez were converted into a royal domain and integrated into the system of palaces and country estates making up the Royal Patrimony.

The Royal Springtime Residence

This was the principal function of Aranjuez from the period of Philip II until the last third of the nineteenth century, because the fertility of the land and the benign temperatures made it a pleasant place in which to spend the spring and autumn seasons. The Monarchs would stay there from the end of Holy Week until late June; during the summer they travelled to Valsaín (La Granja de San Ildefonso from the reign of Philip V onwards), and in the autumn they went to the Escorial Monastery. Philip II, who was responsible for regulating all the royal residences and their seasonal use, established the municipal ordinances governing Aranjuez: they stipulated that no one could live in the Royal Residence Town except those dedicated to the care of the King himself, so that even during the Court's expeditions or visits, only those Royal Household employees who accompanied His Majesty could reside there: if private persons, ambassadors included, wished to be near the King, they had to be accomodated in the surrounding towns. This rule was maintained until 1750. Throughout the old régime, and particularly for the literary geniuses of the Spanish Golden Age, Aranjuez was the prime example of natural beauty and the earth's fertility, a species of paradise reserved for the King of Spain: "The Escorial of Art, the Aranjuez of Nature" were, in the words of Gracián, considered worthy of maximum esteem.

Two very different periods of work may be discerned in this model territorial arrangement: the first corresponds to the reign of Philip II, and the second to those of Ferdinand VI and Charles III. The result is a landscape composed of orchards and gardens, aesthetically pleasing while at the same time productive. In Terán's words, the layout "was the

The Palace dam, which retains the Tagus in front of the Royal residence, must be the work of Juan Bautista de Toledo. Its purpose is to regulate the water's entry into the inlet separating the Palace from the Island Garden, and insofar as possible to protect the latter from flooding by the river. It also used to provide energy to a watermill which already existed at the end of the 15th century. In 1828, Ferdinand VII granted a private company the right to exploit the waterfall, and in 1830 a wheatmill was opened, the present appearance of which, altered by subsequent reforms, contrasts with the Palace and Gardens. But this dam is only one among the important **hydraulic works** undertaken in Aranjuez by the House of Austria and the Bourbons; notable is the Dam or "Sea" of **Ontígola**, built by the Dutch engineer Pieter Janson and Juan Bautista de Toledo in 1563-1573, to supply the fountains of the Island Garden. Its technical characteristics - buttresses, embankment and capacity - made it a pioneer work of 16th-century engineering. The **Dam of Sotomayor** (or del Embocador), begun around 1530, is the key to the irrigation system of Aranjuez, since both the principal irrigation canals built in the reign of Philip II flow from it: the Caz (irrigation canal) de Sotomayor (or de las Aves) on the left bank of the Tagus, and the Caz del Embocador (or de la Azuda) on the right bank. The **Valdajos Dam**, 1530, was built to allow the water of the Tagus to enter the old Acequia (irrigation ditch) de Colmenar (or de Tajo).

The Palace and Parterre reflected in the waters of the River Tagus, retained by the Palace dam.

Juan Bautista de Toledo is a crucial figure in Spanish architecture; he was called from Italy by Philip II to design and direct the construction work the King had decided to undertake, which was to establish a Classical architectural image for the Monarchy. Apparently born in Madrid, he worked as an assistant to Michelangelo (1546-1548), at St.Peter's in the Vatican. Then, under the orders of the Viceroy Pedro de Toledo, he did some important work in Naples from 1548 until 1559, when Philip II recalled him to Spain: he was active in Aranjuez until his death in 1567. His role was transcendental in the introduction of the Classical forms of the late Renaissance to the Spanish Court. The *Palace of Aranjuez* is one of his principal contributions in this respect, since it is a *villa* or country mansion, a type of building carried to a high degree of perfection by the Italian architects of the period. In Spain, this type of building had only one precedent on such a scale, and even larger - the Palace of Charles V in Granada, destined to be the *villa regia* of "His Caesarean Majesty" just as Aranjuez would be that of "His Catholic Majesty" Philip II, the "Prudent King;" both buildings were left unfinished in their lifetimes. The Escorial Monastery, Toledo's most important project, was also not completed in accordance with his plans, being finished but only with major modifications.

In Aranjuez, Juan Baustista de Toledo was also responsible for the layout of the Island Garden and the cultivated lands, with the grand designs of the Picotajo, Doce Calles, and Calles de la Reina and de Toledo. These schemes are related to the somewhat later town-planning projects of Pope Sixtus V in Rome, and are a prelude to the later Baroque parks.

result not of the free and spontaneous occupation and transformation of the workable land, but rather of one controlling will and a rational plan."

Nature subjected to control by Philip II: tree-lined avenues, gardens and orchards

Philip II proposed carrying out the project of his father, Emperor Charles V, to turn Aranjuez into a royal seat, by constructing a new Palace and service buildings, organising the territory by means of a system of straight tree-lined avenues, making use of the available water by means of dams and canals to irrigate orchards and gardens, and rationalization of the cultivated areas. Some of these initiatives had already been started under the Masters of Santiago and Charles V, including the Sotomayor dam on the River Tagus, from whence flowed the principal canals and irrigation ditches. Nevertheless, Philip II is considered the instigator of the general programme, which involved not only various engineers, but also the prominent architect Juan Bautista de Toledo.

Thus, the reign of Philip II saw major hydraulic works and the layout of gardens on the fertile valley floor, employing a typically "Mannerist" geometrical design of straight tree-lined avenues, directly related to Juan Bautista de Toledo's town-planning projects in Naples and to those of Domenico Fontana in Rome. As such, it was a precursor of later designs of Baroque parks. The areas covered by these avenues were, basically, the diamond-shaped space to the west of the Palace, the Picotajo orchards, the Doce Calles, Calle de la Reina and other smaller ones in the Sotomayor area. The King ordered systematic agricultural cultivation of these and other areas, and had new orchards created, such as the "Huerta de los Negros" - part of what is now the Prince's Garden - and those around the nucleus of the palace designed by Juan Bautista de Toledo: the Island Garden, the New Royal Household and the Casa de Oficios.

The dams, irrigation ditches and other hydraulic works were fundamental to Aranjuez, given the character of the Royal Seat and the importance of agriculture in its development. They served particularly to channel the water to irrigate the fertile valley lands, but also to restrain the force of the river's currents so as to avoid possible damage to the crops on the fertile land. Furthermore, use was made of the dams to establish watermills and build bridges. Without doubt, the most interesting project was the attempt to make the River Tagus navigable, a scheme on which Philip II employed the architect Juan Bautista de Toledo and his best engineers. But this utopia was not feasible then, nor later during the reign of Charles IV, when the architect Villanueva was asked to study its viability.

Though the buildings of the Palace and adjoining facilities (continued by the architects Herrera, Gili and Minjares after Toledo's death) were left unfinished until the 18th century, Philip II and his

architects had already established the essential elements and the guidelines to be followed in any future development of the Royal Seat. During the seventeenth century the layout of Aranjuez, as conceived and executed during the reign of Philip II, was carefully maintained and did not undergo any changes or innovations of interest: though the remaining Kings of the House of Austria, particularly Philip IV, held celebrated entertainments there, they did not introduce any important changes, but continued the construction of the Casa de Oficios and had new fountains and statues installed in the gardens. The initiative to continue construction of the Palace was a failure, and only some decorative elements were added. Another initiative of Philip IV was equally unsuccessful, namely the foundation of a Benedictine monastery in the Domain, with a series of scattered hermitages which would have converted the royal forest into a species of religious "wilderness", or a Mannerist "sacred park" in the style of the Buen Retiro in Madrid.

The Bourbons: Royal Aranjuez, model of a Court town and a great agricultural undertaking

After the end of the War of Succession, in 1715 Philip V undertook the completion of the Palace, which was later enlarged by Charles III. The first Spanish Bourbon King also arranged for the construction of some of the auxiliary buildings and introduced significant innovations in the gardens, both those already existing and new ones such as the Parterre, the Islet and the now vanished Queen's Garden. However, it was his son, Ferdinand VI, who not only made Aranjuez the scenario of

Anonymous seventeenth-century painting: A bird's eye view of Aranjuez around 1630. Prado Museum.

Giacomo Bonavia's plan for Aranjuez (1749) corresponds to criteria more luxurious than functional, inasmuch as it makes a compromise between the network of city blocks and the emphatic trident, of Roman and Versaillesque influence, formed by the tree-lined streets of la Reina, Príncipe and Infantas. Perpendicular to the axis of the trident, that of the great Plaza de San Antonio is established, on the line of the entrance and the Andalusia highway.

Aranjuez became a model agricultural undertaking of the Enlightenment during the reign of Charles III, who established here what could be called "truly royal agriculture" (Ponz). "Desirous of encouraging agriculture in the kingdom by all means...he wanted to offer his subjects a royal example at this Residence which would serve them as an superior incentive...he did not spare expense in sowing great areas and plantations, experimenting for public utility" (Quindós). The layout of the cultivated land is more luxurious than profitable; above all, its value is representative, as an image of the ideal of the country desired by the enlightened Monarchy, and as the expression of the ideology of power. The new tree-lined avenues unite and articulate the various agricultural undertakings, and constitute a coherent and organic evolution of the system created under Philip II. The Cortijo and the Flemish Field stand out. The plan and views of Domingo de Aguirre reflect the maximum splendour of this rural magnificence of the Crown, the system of tree-lined avenues inherited and expanded, the apogee of the cultivations of the Residence and the new buildings constructed for this purpose.

This vast model undertaking of the Enlightenment would be maintained by the Crown during the reigns of Ferdinand VII and Isabel II, but was then dismembered under the 1869 legislation. Under the law of 1982 governing the Patrimonio Nacional, the tree-lined avenues of the Royal Residence Town ceased to belong to the Patrimonio Nacional, being transferred to the Patrimony of the State in 1988.

sumptuous festivals directed by the castrato Farinelli, but also gave the Royal Seat a new dimension. he created a small Court town where any of the court followers could reside, perfectly organized according to a plan drawn up by the architect Giacomo Bonavia, with regular city blocks, wide streets and tree-lined promenades. The most outstanding elements in the town plan of Aranjuez, and possibly the most important ones in 18th-century Spanish urban planning (together with the Barceloneta district of Barcelona), are those that united the palace nucleus with its environment - the great porticoed Plaza de San Antonio, and the trident formed by the avenues extending from the Palace Parterre and passing through both the urban and the cultivated areas.

Charles III not only continued with his stepbrother's schemes, to the point of making Aranjuez a model of the Enlightenment town proposed to the country by the Court, and erected new buildings such as the Theatre, San Carlos Hospital and San Pascual Convent; he also extended the gardens, cultivated areas and tree-lined boulevards. The King made the whole Domain an example of the rational agricultural undertaking that the Enlightened Despotism wished to be the economic basis of the State. Within this general programme may be included developments such as the Real Cortijo de San Isidro, the Campo Flamenco, the Huerta Valenciana, and Los Deleites...The irrigation system inherited from the 16th century was considerably improved in the 18th century; during the reign of Ferdinand VI, the engineers Charles de Witte and Leonardo de Vargas worked to upgrade the existing system.

Besides finishing the Long Bridge and beginning the Queen's Bridge, consolidating the security of the river crossings with these and other solid constructions, Charles III improved the irrigation network with canals designed to water the Royal Cortijo or farmland.

The Prince's Garden also came into being during the reign of Charles III, when he introduced improvements to the pre-existing orchards. After Charles IV came to the throne, he enlarged it and built the Real Casa del Labrador at one edge of the property. Private initiatives completed the splendours of the town, with the construction of aristocratic residences including that of the Prime Minister Manuel Godoy, whose clamorous downfall came in the Aranjuez Revolt of 19th March 1808, an immediate prelude to the Napoleonic invasion and subsequent war.

The full extent and development of the Royal Domain of Aranjuez at the end of the 18th century is reflected in the general plan and views, all surveyed and drawn in 1773 under the supervision of the engineer Domingo de Aguirre, and engraved in Madrid's Royal Calcography. And so it was maintained for a century, until the Disentailment Law led to the transfer of much of the land into private hands. The moment of maximum splendour for Aranjuez was the reign of Charles IV: it was his

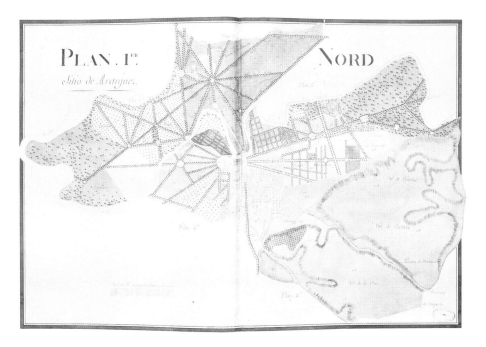

favourite Royal Residence, and he stayed there not only during the spring months of May and June, but also during the earlier months of the year, which his predecessors, particularly his father, usually spent at the Palace of El Pardo.

Santiago Loup: Section 1 of the planimetric map of Aranjuez, 1811. I.G.N.

The Nineteenth and Twentieth Centuries

Ferdinand VII brought back the sparkle to the springtime "expeditions" and to Aranjuez. The reign of Isabel II was the last period of Court splendour for this Royal Seat, where palaces were built for some members of the Royal Family - the Queen Mother's in El Deleite, one for Prince Adalbert of Bavaria - and for the old and new aristocracies - the Oñate, Tamarit, Narváez and Salamanca families - almost all located to the southeast of the royal dwelling, the majority now vanished. The touch of Isabel II in Aranjuez is noted in the decoration of many of the rooms in the Royal Palace. But, without doubt, the principal innovation took place in 1851, when Spain's second railway line arrived in Aranjuez, mutilating a large number of the tree-lined avenues in Picotajo and in the square to the west of the Royal Palace, due to the desire to situate the railway station as close as possible to the Royal Palace and to the town.

The 1868 revolution and the following six-year period, when the policy of disentailment of Crown estates was applied, brought about

"I liked the town of Aranjuez as much as the palace, the garden and the park. All the green-shuttered houses are new and white, and the avenues are all straight. The King hands over the land free to anyone who wants to build, as long as they abide by the original city plan which imposes great unity upon the buildings. There is not a more orderly town in the entire world and it continues to grow...The King and court spend the months of May and June here...the most select people from Madrid have built their own residences here to honour the Monarch, who prefers Aranjuez to the other Royal Residences, and in my opinion, he is right." Joseph BARETTI. *A Journey from London to Genoa...*,[1760], London, 1770.

The Plaza de San Antonio is the key to the Bonavia's city plan, since it forms the link between the royal residence and the town; it establishes a balance between the palace axis, running east-west, made up of avenues branching out from the Palace with scenic perspectives, and the north-south axis of the Plaza and the highway from Madrid to Andalusia. The palatine area is to the east of the Plaza; to the west and south is the town. The most notable architectural features of the Royal Residence Town surround the Plaza: the principal houses for the Royal entourage and servants, the town Chapel, the stables and armoury, the theatre...The northern side is open to the river and the gardens, so establishing a relationship between the Court and urban scenarios.

Bonavia intended to prolong the curved arcades up to the corners of the city blocks formed by the Caballeros and Infantes streets, concealing the avenue entrances. Marquet, by tearing down some of the side arches - two on each side, it seems - turned the Plaza's corners into right-angles and built four big "carriage gateways" to mark the avenue entrances. The evidently French style of these lowered archs, delicately bolstered, and the change in scale between these new elements and the side arches and porticoes flanking them, reveal the work to be by Marquet. This variation, by emphasizing rather than hiding the circulation axes at the end of the plaza, effects a total change in the the concept of the space.

important changes in property ownership, with the massive sale of land and buildings belonging to the Royal Patrimony. This is the principal reason why the Royal Seat of Aranjuez was abandoned by subsequent Monarchs: the Bourbon restoration in the person of Alfonso XII did not mean that Aranjuez was once again the spring scenario for the powerful, who had already adopted a newer fashion, being satisfied with a summer break in San Ildefonso, or on the beaches of the North. The "expeditions" of the intermediate seasons became relics of the past. Since then, Monarchs have only visited Aranjuez for fleeting one-day excursions.

The transfer of land into private hands at the end of the 19th century favoured economic growth based on agriculture. The Royal Seat of the Bourbons reached the mid-20th century with all its architectural and landscape elements preserved; since then, however, it has been considered more advantageous for Aranjuez to encourage its growth as an industrial centre rather than to foster its ecological, landscape and historical values. Development-orientated policies considered industrialization more profitable for the town than promotion of its possibilities as a centre of attraction for tourism of greater qualitative importance. Over forty years ago, in *Madrid y Sitios Reales,* the architectural historian Chueca Goitia pointed out that "it is urgent to formulate a plan to save Aranjuez." The re-routing of the main highway to Andalusia away from the town centre has, however, reduced the negative effects of traffic.

Recently, by virtue of the Law of 1982 governing the Patrimonio Nacional, all the tree-lined avenues and rural properties still managed by Patrimonio Nacional in Aranjuez, in addition to some buildings which were declared unrelated to the Royal Palace complex, were transfered to the State Patrimony. Consequently, Patrimonio Nacional, successor entity to the former Royal Patrimony of the Crown, now administers only the Royal Palace with its Island Garden and the Parterre, the Casa de Oficios and Casa de Caballeros, the Royal Church of San Antonio, the Prince's Garden, the Casa del Labrador and the Royal Convent of San Pascual.

ARRIVAL IN ARANJUEZ

Something of what was signified by these qualities of the royal country seat par excellence may be appreciated when arriving in Aranjuez from Madrid. If we take the Calle de Toledo, one of the main streets designed by Philip II, it leads directly to the principal façade of the Royal Palace. But for those who have come on the old Andalusia highway, it is the remains of the 18th-century image that meet the eye. After crossing the Long Bridge spanning the River Jarama, built by the engineer Marcos de Vierna and finished in 1761 under Charles III, we continue along what

were once long avenues of linden trees laid out on the initiative of Fernando VI, the Calle Larga and the Calle del Rey; then we traverse the central square of the Doce Calles, and after crossing the River Tagus enter the town itself.

The Plaza de San Antonio

This is the first magnificent urban scenario in Aranjuez where the Bourbon Court displayed its magnificence during the springtime. The plaza was conceived by the architect Bonavia as a setting for the statue of King Ferdinand VI which used to surmount the fountain, giving the plaza an emblematic character. It is flanked by buildings for the royal retinue: the Casa de Oficios and Casa de Caballeros to the right, the Casa de Infantes to the left, all surrounded by galleries attached to the Palace and modelled on the 16th-century Casa de Oficios. To give architectural definition to the Plaza's wide open space, the far end

Plaza San Antonio with the Venus Fountain, also known as the "Mariblanca Fountain."

The Royal Church of San Antonio was conceived in 1750 by Bonavia, in such a way that "it faces onto and gives perspective to the middle section of the end of the new plaza, where the fountain is to be placed..." Conceived from the very beginning as a rotunda with a dome crowned by a lantern, the project for the façade and galleries which were to join it to the long sides of the Plaza, was modified by the architect himself early in 1751. It was finished on 13th March 1753.

The Plaza's fountain, as originally conceived by Bonavia, was inspired by another similar monument, erected in honour of a sovereign of the Spanish Monarchy, Charles II, in the capital of one of his kingdoms, Naples: the fountain in the Piazza Monteleone by Fanzago and Caffaro (1667-1672). The statue of Ferdinand VI in Carrara marble that Olivieri had carved in Madrid, was placed here on 8th April 1752, in such a way that his gaze is directed toward the "royal highway and the gardens"; shortly afterwards were added the three lions still decorating the fountain's base.

In 1760, Charles III deprived the fountain and the Plaza of their political and iconographic meaning, when he ordered the removal of his stepbrother's statue, which is now in Madrid's Plaza de Paris; in its place he installed a Venus carved by Juan Martínez Reina, and inspired in a similar figure on a fountain that used to be in Madrid's Puerta del Sol, the so-called "Mariblanca", and by this same name she is known in Aranjuez. The shell on the fountain may be considered as a symbol of the fertility that water offers to the district. No change to the fountain's architectural structure was made under Charles III, but in 1831 Ferdinand VII decided to "modernize" its Baroque structure, its present form being due to Isidro González Velázquez. The combination of the battlemented tower and the lions gives the fountain a heraldic feel, a precedent for which can be found in the fountain erected by Sacchetti in 1754 in front of Madrid's City Hall.

needed a strong element, which was to be the charming late baroque façade of the Royal Church of San Antonio, connected by colonnades with the Caballeros and Infantes galleries. These rounded arches unify the Plaza's volumes and parts. The trees serve to bring the considerable width of the Plaza into proportion with the low buildings surrounding it, and to produce a continuum between the tree-lined streets within the town and outside it and the gardens. The Garden of Isabel II is another mass of trees, occupying an unbuilt city block that possibly would have restricted the sensation of unity with the whole. The harmony of the Plaza is based on the balance between these axes and the architectural elements.

The Plaza was given its definitive configuration during the reign of Charles III, when the Casa de Caballeros was finished and the Casa de Infantes was built opposite, the arches linking the colonnades of these buildings and the lateral wings of San Antonio Church were erected, and the Plaza was again levelled and the trees removed. All these schemes were designed by Jacques Marquet, and supervised by the overseer Manuel Serrano, in the absence of the French architect.

The Fountain in the Plaza de San Antonio was designed in 1750 as a tribute to the reigning King, Ferdinand VI, giving this urban space the character of a Royal Plaza, and creating the proper scenario to glorify the Monarch responsible for the entire plan. Besides its monumental character, the fountain also fulfilled a function worthy of note: the supply of drinking water to this new town. The fountain has undergone many transformations in its history, and reflects two interlinked architectural projects, the first dating from 1750, and the second from the remodelling of 1830, which gave rise to its present appearance. There are also two iconographic readings to the sculptures, the original one of 1750 and that of 1760.

The Plaza is separated from the river by the Palace *Parterre*, or ornamental flower garden, in front of which is the trident shape formed by the streets of la Reina, el Príncipe and las Infantas.

THE ROYAL PALACE AND ITS GARDENS

The Parterre is entered through the front gate, opposite the trident, or through the small doorway below the arches communicating the gallery of the Casa de Oficios with the Palace gallery: in this way the visit can begin with the Palace Gardens. However, to enter the Royal Palace itself one should walk along under the Palace colonnades, and pass the façade onto the Plaza de las Parejas, so reaching the oval explanade known as "Raso de la Estrella," where five tree-lined avenues converge, among them Calle de Toledo.

The *Raso de la Estrella*, with its elegant benches made of Colmenar limestone, owes its present form (1780) to the architect Francisco

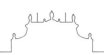

Sabatini. It is the logical consequence of the enlargement of the Royal Palace with two additional wings designed by the same architect on the instructions of Charles III.

The Royal Palace

The two wings built by Sabatini contain the *Royal Chapel* and the Theatre. They were finished, respectively, in 1775 and 1778, and form a French-style "courtyard of honour" known as the *Plaza de Armas*, closed by a modern gate that follows Sabatini's project just as it appears in the engraving by Domingo de Aguirre. The Palace's *principal front*, so unitary in appearance, incorporates architectural elements spanning almost two centuries. The central section, with a portico and façade surmounted by sculptures of *Philip II, Philip V* and *Ferdinand VI,* by G. D. Olivieri (1748), is by Bonavia and dates from the reign of Philip V, as does the left-hand sector with the dome of the old theatre, while the right section, with the matching dome of the old chapel, dates back to the reign of Philip II.

The original project of architect Juan Bautista de Toledo offered a curious solution to the Renaissance theme of the *villa regia*, a country seat for the King's relaxation. As a palace, it is conventional in its central patio layout and the formality of its façade. However, its character as a *villa* is revealed by its open design: both the main façade and the side ones facing onto the gardens had ground-floor arcades, which later were walled in and replaced by windows. At the same time, this area was isolated from the exterior by the "enclosed gardens"

The main façade of the Royal Palace with the wings surrounding the Courtyard of Honour designed by Sabatini; view from the Raso de la Estrella.

The Grand Dauphin, son of Louis XIV, by Antoine Coizevoix.

Louis XIV, by Antoine Coizevoix.

The history of the construction of the Palace explains the distance in time between the various parts, as well as their similarities and differences. In 1563 Philip II entrusted the project to his architect Juan Bautista de Toledo, but when Toledo died in 1567 hardly more than the foundations of the Chapel had been laid. His disciples Gili and Herrera continued the construction until 1577, completing the Chapel, the right-hand section of the main façade, and the wing between the Courtyard of Honour and the King's Garden, as well as this Garden itself. When this was finished, representing scarcely half the Palace, Philip II stopped the construction to give preference to other works, and so the Palace remained until the beginning of the 18th century, although in 1636 Philip IV did commission his architect Juan Gómez de Mora to continue. It was this architect who, for the first time, proposed a change in the original project and the introduction of a grand staircase, though this was not built due to lack of funds. In 1715, Philip V ordered the Palace to be completed; the Master of Works of Aranjuez, Pedro Caro Idrogo, under the remote supervision of the Master of the Royal Works, Teodoro Ardemans, built all the east wing, followed by the north and the west wings, which make up the left-hand section of the main façade. Idrogo, far from reproducing with exactitude the first half already built, introduced important modifications in the groundplan, to the point that the north wing is wider than the south wing. Giacomo Bonavia, who was in charge of the works from 1735 onwards, finished the new part of the façade and all the central section, with the staircase which was begun in 1743-44. In 1752 the last details were finished, after repairs to the roofs destroyed by a fire in 1748.

surrounding it. Altogether, this style was characteristic of the art of the Court of Philip II, which mixed specifically Spanish features with Italian Mannerist influences. The classical design of its façades and architectural details corresponds to the style in vogue in Rome during the mid-16th century. Various reasons, among them the similarity of the groundplan of the King's Quarters and the so-called "grill-handle" layout at the Escorial Monastery, suggest that this 16th-century project for the Royal Residence of Aranjuez, as we know it from 17th-century plans and ideal representations, was conceived as a whole and designed by the architect Juan Bautista de Toledo; but there are still doubts about the additions and modifications possibly executed by his disciples, particularly Juan de Herrera. The most notable reform carried out on the 16th-century part during the 18th century was the division of the galleries into habitable rooms, especially that of the old Chapel - which used to be in in the clock tower overlooking the *Plaza de las Parejas* - when Sabatini built the new one.

The Main Staircase

The vast box of the staircase occupies the entire bay between the façade and the patio: in the 17th century, the architect Gómez de Mora had already thought of building a monumental staircase here, and then Caro Idrogo projected a very original one with two curved flights of steps, but the project was never finished. At the end of the reign of Philip V, between 1743 and 1746, Giacomo Bonavia constructed this grandiose imperial staircase, enriched with diverse entrances in the initial flights, which are displayed in a theatrical manner characteristic of a Northern Italian late-Baroque scenographic

taste. The effect is very noble, although it is detrimental to the whole that the ceiling was never decorated. It is not surprising that Bonavia, encouraged by the protection of the Queen's Secretary and by the success of this staircase, aspired to having a project of his adopted for the Royal Palace in Madrid. The magnificent wrought-iron rococo balustrade with gilded bronze decoration is the work of Francisco Barranco and collaborators. The wide steps are made of single blocks of white limestone from the nearby town of *Colmenar de Oreja*, the magnificent quality of which made it widely used not only in Aranjuez but also in Madrid from the 16th century onwards, and particularly in the 18th century.

In the vaulted niches on the main landing are displayed three works by the Sun King's principal sculptor, Antoine Coisevoix: busts of *Louis XIV*, his wife María Teresa of Austria and their son, the **Grand Dauphin**, father of Philip V. With the rest of the Dauphin's "jewels" (the most important pieces are in the Prado Museum), these sculptures, signed and dated 1638 except for that of the King, passed into the Spanish Royal Collections. On the upstairs landing, over the balcony, is the *Equestrian Portrait of Alfonso XIII*, by

The Royal Palace's main staircase, by Giacomo Bonavia.

Ideal View of the Aranjuez Palace: anonymous Madrid artist. El Escorial Monastery.

Giacomo Bonavia is the architect who has most influenced the appearance of Aranjuez, since he designed and directed the works for the conclusion of the Royal Palace, with its principal staircase, the layout of the town, the Plaza and Chapel of San Antonio, and many other buildings in Aranjuez, where he worked until his death in 1759. Born at Piacenza (Italy), city of the Duchy of Parma where Queen Isabella Farnese was born, his formation was in the northern Italian school of trompe l'oeil painting and scenographic architecture derived from the Bibiena family. He came to Spain in 1728 as assistant to his master, G. B. Galluzzi, in painting the ceilings with trompe l'oeil architectural designs and other interior decoration schemes, including the Queen's Lobby of the Palace that no longer exists as Charles III had the Porcelain Room installed there. At the end of the reign of Philip V he began to design architectural projects, becoming director of works at the Royal Residence in 1745. Protected by the Queen's Secretary, the Marqués Scotti of Piacenza, he carried out important work for the Court in both Aranjuez and Madrid.

Ceiling of the King's Bedroom: architectural decorations by Bonavia and figures by Rusca.

Herreros de Tejada. The large white marble vases in the niches are from La Granja and date from the 18th century, as do the busts on the opposite side.

When the new railway line from Madrid to Aranjuez was inaugurated on 16th March 1850, a branch line brought the royal carriage directly to the foot of the staircase.

Through the right door of the wide upper landing, one enters what during the 18th century were the King's Apartments, later converted for the use of Isabel II as she was the Queen Regnant. Her consort, Francisco de Asís de Borbón, occupied the suite formerly reserved for the Queen: these rooms are entered through the left-hand door on the main landing. They belong to the part of the Palace built in the 16th century: until Philip V, they were the King's rooms - those of the Queen being in the old palace of the Grand Masters of Santiago.

Charles IV introduced significant changes in the layout, joining some rooms together so as to make larger ones. The decoration undertaken during his reign was very important, but since the overall image of the complex is Isabelline, one should bear in mind that the eighteenth-century ceilings and fixed decorations seen in the Queen's Apartments were made for the King's use, and vice versa.

Due to the season of the year in which it was used, this Palace was never decorated with tapestries but with pictures on top of the silk hangings. The painting collection was important, but it varied over time: it was augmented during the reign of Charles III, when four hundred works were brought from the Escorial Palace, and even more were added under Charles IV, who ordered the same number of works to be brought from La Granja. These artistic riches later went to the Royal Museum, the Prado, during the reign of Isabel II, while some of the pictures that were left behind were later sent to other Royal Palaces.

Unless otherwise indicated, all the furniture of mahogany and gilded carving is from the period of Ferdinand VII (first third of the 19th century), as are the French bronze gilt candelabra and clocks bought by the same King; the carved doors are from the period of Ferdinand VI, dated towards 1750; the Czech crystal lamps are modern, from the 1960s, as are the large marble paving stones of the floor. Since the Isabelline period was the last time when the Palace was really used by the Monarchs, the image and names of this epoch have prevailed. In that time, specifically during the years 1850-52, a major redecoration campaign was undertaken, the influence of which has not been eliminated by the modifications dating from the reign of Alfonso XIII or other subsequent restorations. However, almost all the contemporary paintings that used to hang in the rooms of Isabel II, and above all in those of her husband who was very fond of art, have since been moved elsewhere.

The Guard Room

Until the 20th century the decoration of this room was much more austere, no paintings being hung there, but with two large engraved maps: a view of Aranjuez by Aguirre, and another of Naples by the Duke of Noja, which now hangs on the ground floor. Now seen here is the work of Franz Snyders, *Dogs attacking a Stag*. Also the splendid Venetian-style paintings by Luca Giordano: *Solomon annointed King*, *Solomon inspired by Jehova*, and *Solomon and the Queen of Sheba*. Outstanding is the map cabinet of olive-wood and bronze gilt from the period of Charles IV; an Isabelline bronze clock with auxiliary pieces, and the French Empire-style vases.

The Queen's Lobby

Important paintings by Luca Giordano are in this room, such as *Triptolemus, Jupiter and Leda, Aeolus,* and *The Arrest of Christ;* in addition to the work by Vicente Carducho, *The Death of San Juan de Mata.*

Solomon and the Queen of Sheba by Luca Giordano.

Antechapel of the Royal Palace: View of the Roman Forum, made in the Vatican mosaic workshops.

Patron saints of the Prince of Asturias (Alfonso XII), 1862, in the Antechapel of the Royal Palace.

Our Lady of Sorrows from the Vatican mosaic workshop, after a model by Carlo Maratta, papal gift to María Amalia of Saxony in 1738.

The Queen's Antechamber

Two oil paintings in this room show scenes of *The Story of the Prodigal Son*, attributed to Signorelli (Italian school, first half 17th century). Also works by Francesco Solimena, *Eucharist with the Virgin and St.Dominic*, and *San Juan de Capistrano*, *San Buenaventura* and *Santa Coleta*. Clocks in the Louis XVI style, one signed by Imbert the elder and the other by Guydamour.

In the rooms through which we have already passed, including this one, the carved wooden doors date from the reign of Philip V and the marble floors are by the architect Andrada, dating from 1962-63.

The Queen's Chamber or the Queen's Music Room.

Outstanding works from the School of Furini are: *Lot led out of Sodom guided by Angels; Charles III with the Cloak of his Order,* a modern copy of the original by Maella conserved in the Royal Palace in Madrid; and *Isabel II*, an anonymous oval painting. The two big twin mirrors also date from her reign. A tapestry from the *Dido and Aeneas* series, woven in Brussels at the end of the 16th century. A piano by Collard and Collard (prize-winners in the 1849 London exhibition) bought by Isabel II for the Porcelain Room. Two twin console tables from the reign of Ferdinand VII have marble tops encrusted with marine fossils, and the third is similar to that in the Queen's Lobby, made of Espejón marble. From this room onwards, all the doors belong to the period of Charles IV. In all of these rooms the draperies are modern.

Antechapel

Paintings by Corrado Giaquinto: *St. Antony of Padua*; and *the Virgin with St. Ferdinand*, *St. Barbara and St. Cecilia*. These two paintings are interesting, the first because it was painted as the reredos of a side altar for the original Chapel of this Palace; and the second because the patron saints of King Ferdinand VI and Queen Barbara, great lovers of music, are portrayed next to the patron saint of this art. Vicente Palmaroli, *The Patron Saints of the Prince of Asturias* - later Alfonso XII - dated in Rome, 1862. The mosaics of semi-precious stones from the Vatican hard-stone workshops were papal gifts for royal weddings. Those of Ecce Homo, and Our Lady of Sorrows, after original canvases by Guido Reni, with rich bronze frames imitating the French rococo style, were given by Clement XII to María Amalia of Saxony in 1738, on her marriage to the King of Naples (later Charles III of Spain); the remainder, Flower Vase, St.Peter in Prison, View of the Roman Forum and View of St.Peter's Square, were gifts from Leo XIII to King Alfonso XII and María Cristina of Habsburg-Lorraine in 1879. In this same technique, and considerably superior in quality, is the *Shipwreck* in the style of Vernet. *The Equestrian Statue of Alfonso XII*, commemorating

Ceiling fresco by Francisco Bayeu in the Oratory of Charles IV.

the King's entrance into Barcelona on 8 January 1875, is by R. Elías, dated in 1878. The wall-paper is characteristic of the reign of Alfonso XII. The bronze chandelier is neogothic.

Oratory of Charles IV (called the Queen's Oratory due to its function in the reign of Isabel II)

This was built between 1790-91 under the supervision of Juan de Villanueva, following Francisco Sabatini's design, with stuccos by the Brilli brothers, bronzes by Ferroni and frescoes by Francisco Bayeu on the walls and ceilings, all relating to the Virgin. Above the altar, the *Immaculate Conception* by Maella; Bayeu's frescoes on the side of the balcony represent *The Visitation* and *The Flight into Egypt*; flanking the room, looking toward the altar on the left, is *St. John on Patmos* and to the right, *Solomon*; on either side of the arch, *St. Matthew* and *St. Luke*. All of these have inscriptions with scriptural phrases referring to the Mother of God. In the dome, *The Eternal Father* and three scenes in grisaille: *Birth of Mary, St.Anne and the Virgin as a Girl*, and *The Annunciation*. The mural paintings are inserted into an architectural frame, just as the contemporary tapestries, woven after scenes by Goya and other painters from Bayeu's circle, fitted the walls of the winter palaces at El Escorial and El Pardo; indeed, the stucco moldings imitate the wooden ones used to cover the nails attaching the tapestries to the walls.

"Etruscan" chair after design by J.D. Dugourc. The Queen's Study in the Royal Palace.

The Throne Room.

Isabelline Room

This small room is entered from the Ante-Oratory: it has recently been decorated with pieces from the period of Ferdinand VII and Isabel II. *Woman with Boy* by Luis de la Cruz y Ríos, 1824; three oval pastels representing Isabel's daughters Paz, Pilar and Eulalia as children; the same *Infanta Eulalia* by L. Franco; a young nephew of Francisco de Asís, by Alphonse Muraton; *Isabel II as a child, in the Royal Palace of Madrid, with the Plaza de Oriente and Royal Theatre* in the background, by B. López; and *An Infante*, by an anonymous 18th-century Spanish follower of Mengs. A console table in the style of Ferdinand VII, similar to the one in the Queen's Lobby. From the same period is the pedestal table, and dated somewhat later is the chest-of-drawers; on the table is a plaster bust of *Isabel II as a child*; and above it a bust of *Alfonso XIII as a child*, by Agustín Querol (1892). The chairs are in the style of Alfonso XII. In front of the fireplace, curious Isabelline toy furniture. The stucco socle and marble pavement are old and imitate eighteenth-century models.

Ceiling of the Queen's Study.

The Rococo taste for "Chinoiserie" decoration, of which the Porcelain Room is a typical example, was not greatly concerned with faithfully copying the oriental reality; the exotic suggestions served as an evasion from western society's own classical culture. In this sense, the great enthusiasm of Charles III for "Chinoiserie" is noteworthy, being displayed in works in both Naples and Spain: the Gasparini Chamber in Madrid's Royal Palace is an important example. The similarity between this Aranjuez Porcelain Room and the one of the Portici Palace - now in Capodimonte (Naples) - designed by G.B. Natale in 1759, suggests that Gricci and his team must have been inspired here by designs of the same Piacenza architect and painter, whose protector was Conde Gazzola.

Children's Room

As in the case of the previous room, diverse objects relating to the childhood of the Royal Family during the nineteenth century have been displayed here. The furniture includes three Ferdinand VII changing tables and a pompous chair resembling a throne for Isabel II as a little girl, with her monogram; a walker, a chamber pot and tiny child's high-chair. Among the pictures may be seen a 17th-century Infante; a Boy with a ring-shaped pastry and a toy chair (anonymous Spanish, 18th-century); *Alfonso XIII as a child* (photogravure by Boussod and Valadon, after a drawing by Godin); and *Alfonso XIII and his sisters* by J.Parera, 1888.

The Royal Palace Porcelain Room: detail.

Throne Room

This was the dining room of Charles IV, and from his reign date the two thrones and the stucco floor, but the entire room transmits an impression of the second third of the 19th century, because the furniture and draperies, richly decorated with passementerie and recently restored, are Isabelline in style. The harmony of the green socle and red curtains follows the model of the Throne Room in Madrid's Royal Palace. The ceiling is painted in tempera by Camarón (1850), and depicts an allegory of The *Prosperity of the Spanish Monarchy under Isabel II* - the Royal Crown, supported by Industry, with the Arts, the Spirit of Peace, Abundance, Virtue and Prudence - and in the four medallions at the ends, personifications of the virtues: *Justice*, above the throne, is represented with the Queen's face. The escutcheons display family arms, not those of kingdoms, except for Aragón and León. On the console tables stand six

The Porcelain Room.

The Royal Palace Porcelain Room: detail.

French clocks from the period of Ferdinand VII, two of them outstanding pieces, and two handsome candelabra in the "Egyptian" taste.

The Queen's Study
This was the King's dressing room under Charles IV, when Maella painted the vault with Pompeian motifs and allegories of *Religion, Justice, Abundance and Law*, and scenes of the Passion of Christ. One of the paintings of flowers is by Jon ("Velvet") Brueghel, and the other three are attributed to Juan de Arellano. Two pictures attributed to Francesco Galli Bibiena, *Classical Ruins* and *The Roman Forum with the Arch of Titus*. Alessandro de Anna, two genre scenes. Fernando Ferrant *Landscape*; Julia Alcayde, *Still Life*. R. Atche, bust of Alfonso XII, over the fireplace. Pedestal table of gilt bronze and cut crystal from La Granja. Chairs with "Etruscan" style arms designed by Dugourc during the period of Charles IV.

Porcelain Room
Philip V ordered sumptuous decoration for this room, designed by Galluzzi

and Bonavia, of which the original marble floor survives. The mirrors might also have been brought from Paris. His son Charles, King of Naples, under the influence of his wife, María Amalia of Saxony, founded the famous porcelain manufactory of Capodimonte, from whence workers and even materials were brought with him when he became King of Spain under the title of Charles III. The first work from his new *Royal Porcelain Factory of the Buen Retiro*, and perhaps its masterpiece, was the decoration of this "conversation room" for Charles III, whose monogram appears repeatedly on the porcelain plaques attached by screws onto a wooden frame. The Royal Factory craftsmen directed by José Gricci maintained the same Neapolitan style but surpassed themselves in this room, completed in 1763. Contemporary with the mural decoration are the porcelain chandelier, and chairs designed by José López, based on English models.

The Queen's Bedroom

The ceiling, by Zacarías González Velázquez, portrays the Monarchy accompanied by Justice, the Sciences, the Arts, the Virtues and the Law. It was painted when this room was the study of Charles IV. The furniture forms a set in the style of the French Second Empire, inspired in 18th-century Baroque sources, with rich inlaid decoration. All the furniture was used to decorate the bedroom of Isabel II, not in this Palace but in that of Madrid, from whence they were transferred to Aranjuez at the end of the 19th century. As for the paintings, the *Sacred Heart of Jesus* is by Alejandro Ferrant, and the *Immaculate Conception* by Rafael Tejeo.

The Queen's Bedroom in the Royal Palace. Detail of the canopy, and fresco by Zacarías González Velázquez.

Boudoir of Queen Isabel II.

Ballroom.

Children's Games by Corrado Giaquinto. Gala Dining Room, Royal Palace.

The Queen's Boudoir

The decoration is typical of Victorian taste, and remains exactly as it was after the redecoration carried out between 1850 and 1852, with white grogram draperies adorned by sprays of roses (although the outer white-embroidered tulle curtains are now lost), large mirrors and planters. The ceiling is by Antonio García, also dating from the mid-19th century. The rear doors open onto a water closet and bathroom in the Isabelline style.

Ballroom

Located between the apartments of Isabel II and those of her husband, in the central section of the façade with balconies opening onto the Parterre, this ballroom was also redecorated in the Queen's time, with plaster decoration on the ceiling, mirrors with carved frames, divans and yellow grogram draperies; however, the decoration of the mirror dates from the 18th century, as do the two console tables between the balconies.

Conversation Room

This was both the name and the function given to this room, when it was redecorated in the reign of Ferdinand VI with a magnificent stucco floor, ceiling decorations and paintings, all by Giacomo Amiconi. During the reign of Charles III it formed part of the Prince's Apartments, and later it was used as a Dining Room. The windows look out onto the courtyard of honour. In the centre of the ceiling are represented *Justice and Religion, with Prudence and Charity*, and other virtues to the sides; in the smaller spaces on the end wall, *Eternity* and *Truth*; and painted in grisaille in the angles, the *Four Parts of the World*. This allegorical and moral discourse

alluding to Ferdinand VI - whose face can be identified in the personage of Religion - is reinforced by the paintings above the doors, works in oil by Amiconi and Flipart, which represent virtues associated with the Monarch: *Strength, Harmony, Meekness, Generosity, Humility and Fidelity*. This whole decorative programme including the stucco floor, with musical allegories highly appropiate to Ferdinand VI and Barbara de Braganza, enthusiastic music lovers, is Amiconi's masterpiece in Spain. Of yet higher quality are the large paintings hanging on the walls of this room since the reign of Ferdinand VI, though the rich mahogany and gilt frames are in the style of Ferdinand VII. The pictures are by the Neapolitan artist Corrado Giaquinto, court painter to Ferdinand VI and Charles III, and form part of a series on the *Life of Joseph: Joseph in Prison, The Presentation of Jacob to the Pharoah, The Cup in Benjamin's Bag, Joseph's Triumph, Allegory of Religion, Allegory of Prophecy*, and *Children's Games*. The two large clocks at the ends of the room are from the period of Charles IV, one by

Gala Dining Room.

Dining Room ceiling, detail: fresco painting by Amiconi.

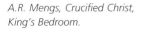

The Arab Room.

"Among many other things I saw a *Crucifixion* by Mengs, not overcharged with expression and with a very delicate palette; the background and sky are sombrely solemn and produce a grandiose chiaroscuro."
William BECKFORD: *Italy with Sketches of Spain and Portugal...*,[1795], London 1834.

Pieter Kenzing (of Neerwinden) and the other by Lépine (Paris). From the same reign are the console tables, designed by Sabatini.

The King's Chamber

Outstanding in this room are the paintings by Fernando Brambilla, part of the extensive series of *Views of the Royal Residences* painted during the reign of Ferdinand VII: *View of the Fountain of Fame* and *The Cascade*, both from La Granja, on either side of the fireplace: and on the opposite walls are views of the Monastery of El Escorial: *The Main Staircase*, *The Pond, The Library, The Courtyard of the Kings, The Sacristy,* and *View from the Gallows Cross.* Also from the period of Ferdinand VII are the console tables, the alabaster ornaments, and the troubadour-style clock, of blued and gilded bronze, which stands on the mantelpiece. From the Isabelline period is the plaster decoration of the ceiling, the Pleyel piano dated after 1855, and the mirror. The antechamber clock is by French of London.

A.R. Mengs, Crucified Christ, King's Bedroom.

The Arab Room

Decorated in 1848-1850 as the smoking room of the King Consort, Francisco de Asís, it is characteristic of the integration of the Nazarí style of Granada into the exotic, historicist repertory of the nineteenth century. Rafael Contreras was selected as the most suitable artist to decorate it because he was in charge of the restoration of the Alhambra, from which he took the "Hall of the Two Sisters" as a basis for this room's decoration. The pedestal table of "Moorish" inspiration, with painted porcelain tiles by Robert (*Boabdil leaving Granada*) and Béranger, was produced in the Royal Factory of Sèvres (1836), a gift from the King of France, Louis Philippe of Orléans, to the Queen Regent María Cristina.

King Francisco's Bedroom

The frescoed ceiling is decorated with architectural trompe l'oeil scenes by Bonavia framing a medallion with *Peace and Justice*, and an allusion to Abundance, all from the period of Philip V. The draperies and canopy, the six stools and the two armchairs in matching upholstery, form a coherent unit in the style of Ferdinand VII, which was already here during the reign of Isabel II. The same is not true of the paintings, however, because twenty-seven works were hung in the room in those days; among those now here are *Christ on the Cross*, by Mengs; two representations of the *Virgin and Child*, one signed by José de Madrazo en 1825, and the other an anonymous Spanish work from the first half of the 18th century; and a Flemish 17th-century *Crucifixion*. The fireplace is Italian, installed here by order of King Francisco de Asís in 1864; above it is a bust of the King signed by Francisco Pérez in 1847; the two vases to the sides are from the Royal

Hall of Mirrors, or Queen María Luisa de Parma's Study, later used as Dressing Room of King Franciso de Asís.

Hall of Mirrors, detail.

Judith with Holofernes' Head by Solimena. King's Study in the Royal Palace.

Music Room of Francisco de Asís: ceiling painted by Juan Duque, detail.

Bureau by Jacob Desmalter, in the King's Study.

Porcelain Factory of La Moncloa, imitating Sèvres works, from the period of Ferdinand VII, with views of the Buen Retiro and the Royal Casino of Madrid. The mirror is also from the same period. The medallions of Isabel II and the King Consort are by Bovet. The bed is characteristic of the Empire style.

Hall of Mirrors

Here was the "gabinete antiguo", which in the reign of Charles II was magnificently decorated by Luca Giordano with tempera and fresco paintings. Their poor condition and changes in taste led in the reign of Charles IV to this Queen's Room being entirely redecorated in the French style, respecting only the fine marble floor dating from the period of Philip V, contemporary with the one in the Porcelain Room. The neoclassical decoration of the Hall of Mirrors was directed by the architect Juan de Villanueva, and executed by the woodcarvers Tomás de Castro and Manuel de Monjas, the gilder Manuel Pérez and the cabinetmaker José López, between 1791 and 1795. Nevertheless, the stylistic affinitites with works by J.D.Dugourc suggest that either he influenced the architect, or the designs are his and Villanueva limited himself to directing the work. The entire room is one of the most finished creations from the period of Charles IV, with a suggestion of the Louis XVI taste. The mirrors, or at least some of them, must be those commissioned in Paris by Philip V. The ceiling paintings with Pompeian motifs date from 1803, by Juan Duque.

Music Room of Francisco de Asis.

David putting on his Armour by Luca Giordano, in the Queen's Guard Room.

The King's Study

From the time of Philip II until the beginning of the 18th century, this room together with all following ones - including two more small rooms with nineteenth-century wall-paper, which are not visited - formed part of the *King's Gallery*, decorated during the period of Charles II with a series of landscape and mythological paintings, principally by the hand of Benito Manuel de Agüero, and now in the Prado Museum. This was the most elaborate decorative programme carried out in the Palace, but Philip V ordered the rooms to be subdivided into smaller ones, and during the time of Charles IV some of the ceilings were repainted, including the one in this room, where Juan Duque represented the *Liberal Arts*. This room was then Queen María Luisa's Chamber. The **secretaire** and console table, by Jacob Desmalter, are masterpieces of French cabinet-making from the late eighteenth century; and the paintings of *Judith* by Solimena and *Solomon and the Queen of Sheba* by Noël Coypel (on either side of the fireplace), are no less fine. The desk and the other pieces of furniture are Empire style from the early nineteenth century. The painting of *Lot and the Angels* is by Furini; the series of works on vellum, *Triumphs of Alexander*, is by Magadán, copies of the engravings by Lebrun. Outstanding among the clocks is an English one of the eighteenth-century, by Shelton, and a French one in Louis XVI style on the mantelpiece. Thirty-two paintings by contemporary artists adorned the walls of this room during the period of Francisco de Asís.

The altarpiece in the Queen's Oratory.

The Royal Palace Chapel viewed from the King's Gallery

King Francisco's Music Room

Juan Duque painted the ceiling during the reign of Charles IV, when this was the Queen's dining room. From this period date the two big ceremonial chairs, notable pieces although they have lost their original upholstery. The chandelier, from the Royal Factory of San Ildefonso, is from the time of Ferdinand VII, and is particularly valued because of the limited number of authentic pieces still preserved. The paintings form part of the series representing *The Prodigal Son*. *St. Matthew*, by Pieter van Mol. The bust of the *Prince of Asturias* - later Alfonso XII - is by Oliva, 1869. During King Francisco's period, no less than eighty-three paintings were displayed here, which together with the furniture provided an example of the decorative overcrowding typical of mid-nineteenth century taste.

Gallery of Chinese Paintings

This series of Chinese paintings on paper is from the first half of the nineteenth century, and was bought by Isabel II in 1847; the works are displayed as they were in 1852, representative of the Isabelline atmosphere that has been lost in other Palace rooms.

The King's Antechamber

Passing from the Music Room to the Chamber by the passage from the staircase reserved for the King's private use, the Antechamber is reached. It has Isabelline wall-paper on the walls and ceiling; the paintings include *Virgin and Child*, in the Murillo style, by Esquivel (1848); *Infante Antonio* and *Ferdinand VII*, both by Vicente López; *Infante Francisco; Moses and Saphora* by Ricca. The four chairs are characteristic of the period of the Queen Regent, and the two inlaid display cabinets are equally typical of the reign of her daughter, Isabel II, whose study they decorated in this Palace.

Queen María Luisa's Oratory

Next to the Antechamber is the Queen's Oratory, with a magnificent canvas by Francisco Bayeu, *Virgin and Child*, in a markedly classical and monumental style. The design of the altarpiece is by Francisco Sabatini: the meticulous marble work, from the Palace workshop directed by Galeotti, and the bronzes by Giardoni.

The King's Guard Room

Before Andrada's reconstruction, aimed at returning the room to its original 16th-century appearance and dimensions, it had long been divided into two parts: the Halberdiers' Room and the King's Lobby. In the latter were hung most of paintings by Luca Giordano now seen here: *Absalom hanging by his Hair from the Tree, Construction of Solomon's Temple, Flight into Egypt, Alfonso XI at the Battle of the River Salado, Battle between Christians and Moors,* and *David putting on his Armour*. The chairs all date from the 18th century, though they are all

different. The showcases contain suits of kings-of-arms and bronze maces from the reign of Ferdinand VII.

The Court Costume Museum has been installed on the ground floor of the Palace, in a space occupied in the eighteenth century by private secretaries and in the nineteenth by various facilities; at present it is being reorganized.

The Royal Chapel

The Chapel was consecrated in 1779, being a characteristic work of the Sicilian architect Francisco Sabatini, who successfully combined the central ground-plan with the protagonism of a tribuna real or royal gallery, from which the King and other royal personages followed the ceremonies. Sabatini also designed the altarpieces, executed by the marble workers from the Palace's royal workshops, with bronzes by Vendetti. He also

The Royal Chapel ceiling with fresco paintings by Francisco Bayeu.

"The Royal Chapel, redone according to the plans of Sabatini, an old Italian architect who enjoyed great favour with Charles III, has merit and is notable for the good distribution of the light, which produces a solemn religious effect. The three altars are noble, and the paintings good."
William BECKFORD: *Italy, with Sketches of Spain and Portugal...,* [1795], London, 1834.

At the beginning of his reign, Philip IV made Aranjuez the scenario of his most brillant festivities, and he decorated it appropriately: in July of 1622, some three hundred statues from the collection of Philip II, which had been in storage in the Alcázar of Madrid, were distributed all around the Aranjuez Palace and Gardens. The placing of one of the series of busts of the twelves Caesars in the niches of the *King's Garden* - just as they were in the Emperor's Garden in the Alcázar of Madrid - also under the King's windows on the southern façade, offered more than a political parallel between both monarchs; they also glorified the dynasty, since on the short side looking east a statue of Philip II, the reigning Sovereign's grandfather (and model) was placed, flanked by the latter's father, Emperor Charles V, and mother Empress Isabel.

The free-standing marble statue of Philip II was preserved in its original 17th-century position until 1986, and at present is under restoration. It is a work by Pompeo Leoni, signed in 1568, probably after a model by his father, Leone Leoni. The small "grotto" in the centre of the niche was transformed in 1622 to receive the statue, and the two grottos immediately adjoining it were closed off to take the medallions of the Emperor Charles V and his wife; these works by Leone were sent to the Prado Museum in 1868. The original series of the Roman emperors was moved during the 18th century, when the wall near the Parterre was demolished; the busts were transferred to the Casa del Labrador. Most of the sculptures brought to Aranjuez by Philip IV were transferred only twelve years later, by order of the King himself, to his new favourite royal residence, the Buen Retiro in Madrid.

directed all the interior decoration, with stuccos by the Brilli brothers, sculptures by Robert Michel, and magificent frescoes by Francisco Bayeu alluding to the Blessed Sacrament and the Virgin Mary. From Maella's hand is the Immaculate Conception on the high altar, now replacing Titian's famous Annunciation. The Descent from the Cross, on the right-hand altar, is a good work from Meng's circle; on the left is a St.Michael by Maella; formerly, another of his works, St.Antony, was hung here.

THE KING'S GARDEN AND THE PALACE PARTERRE

Beneath the gallery connecting the royal residence with the Casa de Oficios, a small door provides access to the Parterre or ornamental garden. In front of the Palace's southern façade, the only one dating back to the 16th century, is the *King's Garden*, which is a perfect example of the "enclosed garden" adorned with statues, a synthesis of the Mudéjar inheritance and of Italian Renaissance influences, so frequently found in Spanish royal palaces of the Habsburgs. This garden and two other similar ones, one to the north and the other flanking the eastern façade, were intended to form a series of *giardini segreti* around the royal residence, similar to those in the Escorial surrounding the King's Quarters. Conceived by Juan Bautista de Toledo, the work was carried out by Juan de Herrera around 1577, and finished in 1582 with the installation of the green jasper fountain carved by Roque Solario. The fountain, and the entire Garden, was restored in 1986. The original brick pavement of the paths was replaced in 1622 by flagstones as we see them now, when Philip IV gave a distinctive character to the garden by replacing some of the grottoes by vaulted niches, and installing a series of sculptures which gave a political-dynastic significance to the garden.

Besides being able to see the garden from his balconies, the King could also contemplate the garden both from the "grottoes" or small rooms situated on the east-facing wall designed to allow him to enjoy the view from a cool and withdrawn place, and from the gallery under the façade, which was an open *loggia* until Philip V ordered it to be sub-divided and the arches closed by walls with windows, in order to provide accomodation for one of his sons. The terrace, built in 1582 over the arcade joining the Palace to the Casa de Oficios, was also conceived as a mirador or vantage point looking out over the garden and the Plaza de las Parejas, which was used for horse-riding displays. Ferdinand VI commissioned Bonavia to build a great platform over the terrace, a monumental royal box for the festivals, but Charles III had it taken down in 1760, returning the terrace to its original state. The immense wall of the Chapel of Philip II reminds us, in its strangely bare aspect, that much of what was designed and projected in the 16th century was never completed. Many liberties were taken with the original project, parts of it unknown, when the Palace was completed in the 18th century.

The small balustrade now enclosing the King's Garden occupies the place of the wall with niches demolished in 1733, in order to incorporate this garden into the new Parterre which was then under construction.

The Parterre was ordered by Philip V in 1727 to a typically French design by the engineer Etienne Marchand. It is a compromise between a parterre in the French manner and the conditioning factors of the site: its position in relation to the Palace, the River Tagus, the bridge and the Casa de Oficios, and the preexistence of the *King's Garden*, the wall of which continued around the entire perimeter of the present Parterre, except on the side of the river. In May of 1730, the gardener Esteban Boutelou was ordered to inspect the land with a view to planting, and during the visit of 1735 the Monarchs could enjoy it from their windows. The restrained river was used here in a picturesque manner as a transition and frontier between wild nature and the area submitted to etiquette: the Parterre's open situation above the water produced, from outside, a sensation of distant accessibility,

The King's Garden.

Jacques Bousseau: a nymph in one of the circular fountains of the Parterre, 1745.

*The Hercules and Antaeus Fountain
in the Parterre Garden.*

**The Casa de Oficios and Casa de
Caballeros** occupy the entire right-
hand side of the Plaza de San
Antonio, and also belong to the
Patrimonio Nacional. **The Casa de
Oficios**, the internal structure of
which was altered in 1949-59, used
to house the kitchens and other
sections of the royal offices for
household and culinary matters, as
well as most of the entourage. It had
already been designed by Juan
Bautista de Toledo, along with the
Palace, but its construction was not
begun until 1584, and then under the
supervision of Juan de Herrera. The
southern side of this building was
called the *Cuarto de Caballeros*
because it was where the entourage
lived.

The Casa de Caballeros, built
around the vast Patio de Cuadrado,
arose as a consequence of the
development of these living quarters
of the royal entourage around a patio
with equal sides, in accordance with a
project by Bonavia, mostly executed
under the direction of Marquet by
Vicente Chornet, in the time of
Charles III.

**The eastern side of the Plaza de
San Antonio** is occupied by the **Casa
de Infantes** and Garden of Isabel II.
The Casa de Infantes was built by
Charles III in 1769 to house the
servants of his sons, the Infantes
Gabriel, Antonio and Francisco Javier.
It is by the site supervisor Manuel
Serrano, who finished it at the end of
1772. The **Garden of Isabel II** was
planted in 1830. A bronze statue
representing Queen Isabel II as a girl
was placed there in 1834, as were
eight stone benches which must have
been brought from the Island, since
they seem to be designed by Sabatini.
The iron railings on a stone base date
from 1844.

appropriate to the image of the King, and from within it allowed the eyes
of the courtiers to wander across an open area free of walls. The same
effect was also extended towards the side of the town, once this had
achieved its definitive appearance as a palatine town and it could be
integrated with the garden and the Palace. For this purpose, in 1760
Charles III ordered the demolition of the continuation of the wall around
the King's Garden, which enclosed the Parterre towards the Plaza, replacing
it by a moat of Colmenar stone, designed and built by the architect Jaime
Marquet. This provided a physical but not a visual barrier, of a type already
used elsewhere in Aranjuez during the reign of Ferdinand VI.

The baroque designs formed by boxwood hedges and flowers were
changed around 1850 by Francisco Viet, following a typical Isabelline
scheme. In 1871-1872 the Parterre was modified to conform to
"modern taste," with sinuous paths forming islets, narrow flower beds
around the ponds and conifers planted to hide the Palace. As it has
come down to us today, the garden is the result of the adulteration of
the original design by three generations of horticulturalists.

The Parterre's fountains were simple water spouts in the 18th century,
but sculpture came increasingly to animate them during the following
century. In 1745, Dumandre placed two lead nymphs sculpted by
Bousseau, painted to imitate firstly bronce and later white marble, in the
two small ponds closest to the Palace. In the central pond he situated a
"swan with children playing round it", substituted at the beginning of the
20th century by the group of Ceres, from the Prince's Garden. In the

circular pond, where a statue of the Tagus was displayed during the 18th century, in 1827 Isidro González Velázquez erected the great fountain of Hercules and Antaeus, with sculptures by Juan Adán, originally intended for a site near the Casa del Labrador. The two sphinxes near the Palace are by Juan Martínez Reina (1750), but this is not their original situation, nor that of the magnificent marble vases, work of French sculptors at La Granja during the reign of Philip V; they were all installed here around 1920.

The Cascade of the Castanets, on the inlet.

The Island Garden

The Palace's northern façade is separated from the Island Garden by a stone-faced inlet of the river which widens into a fan, forming the so-called Cascade of the Castanets, built by Bonavia. The inlet can be crossed by two bridges: the first has steps and dates from 1733; the second began as a simple mouth of the lock through which water could enter from the Tagus, but later a ramp was built on top to allow the passage of the Queen's small three-wheeled carriage, as seen in Battaglioli's paintings showing the festivities of Farinelli. To reach the island it is more evocative to walk down the steps of the first bridge, which links up with the fine Baroque grouping of the *Hercules Fountain*, with its 17th-century ponds and walkways.

The **Island Garden** acquired its definitive structure in 1560, due to Philip II and Juan Bautista de Toledo. The initiative of turning the island into an Italo-Flemish garden originated from the idea of Charles V to select Aranjuez "to found there a rural residence for his recreation", according to a Royal Warrant dated 30 April 1544, extending the terms of another one dated eight years earlier. It was his son, however, during his period as Prince Regent, who began to reorganise the agriculture, irrigation canals and streets. For this purpose he relied on Gaspar de Vega and Alonso de Covarrubias, who in 1550 established the layout of the streets and cross-paths of the gardens and the marble gateways for the orchard.

"The Island is a heavenly place, crossed by avenues and plazas, which in their original state must have been very stiff and formal, but over the last century nature has ruined the regularity of art: the trees have grown beyond the limits set for them, and destroyed the *enfilade* by advancing into the walks, or drawing back from them towards the interior of the squares. The shrubs, not being clipped and trimmed, have grown freely like trees, and dominate the statues and fountains instead of serving them as a modest background, as intended. The terraces and balustrades built along the river are now overgrown with roses and other exuberant shrubs hanging over the current, which is shaded by the crowns of large trees growing on the opposite bank. Many of the statues and groups of the fountains are handsome, some masterly, like those by Algardi. Henry SWINBURNE: *Travels through Spain...*[1776], London 1779.

Detail of a map of Aranjuez by J. Hermosilla. Servicio Geográfico del Ejército.

Hercules Fountain. A 17th-century print.

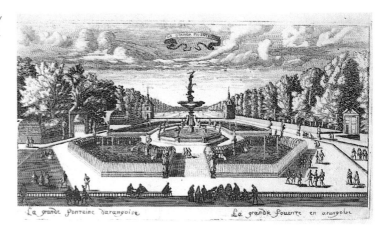

The result of the urban design of Philip II and his grandson's sumptuous contributions, is an original garden that in no way can be compared to the formal French style. The author who perhaps has best defined the greater antiquity of the Island and its different sources of inspiration compared to the classical style of Louis XIV, was precisely one of the French King's courtiers, the Duke of Saint-Simon, who wrote in 1722: "The Tagus surrounds the garden, with a small terrace running along beside the river, which at this point is narrow and not navigable. The garden is large, with a fine parterre and some fine promenades; as for the rest, small groves crossed by low narrow galleries full of fountains with good water adorned with birds, animals and statues that soak the curious when they stop to look at them. The water springs up below their feet; from those artificial birds hanging in the trees an abundant rain falls on them, crossed by further showers from the mouths of the animals and statues, in such a way that one is drowned in a moment without knowing where to find shelter. This whole garden is made according to the old Flemish taste... Accustomed as we are to the good taste of our gardens created by Le Nôtre... one cannot help but find Aranjuez to consist of little, childish things. But overall it proves enchanting and surprising in Castile because of the density of the green shade and the coolness of the waters".

The really decisive phase for the island began in 1560, with the arrival of the architect Juan Bautista de Toledo. In January 1561 the King gave the order to draw up a plan for the garden. Shortly afterwards, some of the first botanical specimens from Flanders and France arrived, in addition to fruit trees from Andalusia and Valencia. Outstanding among the numerous non-Spanish gardeners who worked in Aranjuez, were the Fleming Juan Holvecq and the Italian Jerónimo de Algora, who had worked with Toledo on the Castel Nuovo park in Naples. Although Holvecq wanted the garden to be divided into squares, Juan Bautista de Toledo organised it on the basis of rectangles along the central axis, "because, since the Garden is so long and narrow, the blocks are better proportioned as they are than as squares." The levelling and preparation of the land must have been carried out in 1561, and in the middle of that year the outer walls were begun; these were never really high, but rather were "dykes" or retaining walls on the river-bed. In this way the garden was safe from flooding by the water surrounded it, the principal characteristic of this garden and the reason for its name. By January 1562 the "streets" of the garden had already been levelled, and during 1563 the work progressed rapidly, while at the same time the "Sea of Ontígola" was made to supply the fountains with water. Everything was planted the following year, the small garden plazas were paved with bricks, and the carved marble for the fountains was brought from Italy; their arrangement must be due to Toledo, though their installation did not begin until after his death.

The design of the Island Garden is based on a strong central axis surrounded by rectangular compartments, which in turn are subdivided into squares. The crossings of the principle transversal axes with the central one are marked by small plazas with fountains, arranged along a straight line which simplifies the water distribution while offering a striking perspective. During the 16th and 17th centuries, this central

Hercules and the Hydra Fountain in the Island Garden, seen from the Royal Palace balconies.

"Imagine a park of many leagues, divided in different parts by alleys of two, three and even four miles in extent. Each of these alleys is formed by two double rows of elms, one double row on the right and the other on the left, which provides a deep shade [...] In the middle of each double row there is a narrow channel, through which runs a stream; thus, the trees, even if it does not rain, grow very tall and leafy.
Joseph BARETTI: *A Journey from London to Genoa...* [1760], London, 1770.

avenue was covered by tunnels formed of mulberry trees and wooden trellis-work known as "galleries" or "folías". In this way, a contrast was achieved between the shady spaces on the avenues enclosed by green vaults, and the little plazas inundated by sunshine filtered only by the trees, where the gods of mythology reigned supreme. Small water spouts and hidden jets of water set in the ground along the paths would drench the surprised passerby, who could not escape in the enclosed alley.

As a consequence, varied influences were brought together on the island: the intimacy of Islamic gardens with their low fountains,

The Fountain of the Boy with the Thorn, or "of the Harpies", in the Island Garden.

"Aranjuez has many fine things in its delicious, shady promenades, rivers and gardens. It occupies a lovely plain that descends until reaching the level of the river, hiding itself from the desolate surrounding landscape: a beautiful painting with an ugly and disproportionate frame, an agreeable shady retreat, although not cheerful. There is something melancholic and Moorish in its gardens and buildings; in the places one visits in Spain, it seems to me there is usually something unfinished or in ruins that adds a note of decadence to the whole." Alexander JARDINE: Letters from Barbary, France, Spain, Portugal...,

[1779], London 1790.

Venus Fountain, also known as the Don John of Austria Fountain, Island Garden.

geometric order and proportion, and water games; the enclosed spaces and mythological allusions of the Italian Mannerist garden; and, again, the low Flemish-style parterres of flowers (especially roses, of which Philip II was particularly fond, cultivated here for the distillation of perfumed waters). In 1568, trees were brought from Flanders, by which time the island must already have been finished in the full splendour of its originality. Queen Isabelle de Valois spoke of it as "...ce lieu, qui est le plus beau qu'il est possible...", a phrase seemingly complementary to the words placed on her lips by Schiller in the play *Don Carlos*: "the beautiful days of Aranjuez have passed." The Garden Island's "classical" form is reflected in many engravings from the end of the 17th century, particularly those by Meunier. The transformations that took place on the island during the 18th century, following principles of French landscape gardening, impede our present understanding of this garden of King Philip: the galleries or wooden trellises were removed so that the central axis became a simple tree-lined avenue, and on both sides, the boxwood squares and hedges were given embroidery designs which, with greater or lesser modifications, have come down to us nowadays. The big stone benches or "settees" by Sabatini are splendid, but they greatly modify the original proportions of the little plazas; they were placed there during the reign of Charles III.

The arrangement of the fountains dates from 1582, but their number and richness underwent substantial additions and modifications during the reigns of the son and grandson of Philip II. Particularly important was

The Bacchus Fountain in the Island Garden; the base is by Giambologna, the sculpture by Jonghellinck.

the installation of new fountains undertaken, according to Llaguno, in 1660 by the Master of the Royal Works, Sebastián de Herrera Barnuevo.

The best way to stroll around the Island, at least the first time, is to take the central avenue and then return by the terrace facing the inlet; the map inside the back cover allows identification of the fountains.

The *Hercules Fountain* was erected by Herrera Barnuevo in 1661, apparently where a fountain dedicated to Diana had formerly stood. A conscientious restoration in 1730 did not change its original form. The *Apollo Fountain* is thought to be Neapolitan; perhaps it was sent by the Viceroy Count of Monterrey, but we have no information about its despatch. The 16th-century reliefs on the basin are fine; the sculpture itself is usually attributed to Michelangelo Naccherino (Neapolitan, early 17th century).

The *Fountain of the Hours*, formerly known as *Fountain of the Ring*, is thought to be the oldest one in the garden because of its Hispano-Arab position at ground level; the Roman numerals on the rim have been altered more than once, and originally corresponded to the game of the *Anneau-tournant*, and not a sun dial. In the *Plaza of the Harpies*, the corner niches were built of wood in 1594 to complement the wooden trellises, and being repaired continually they survived until 1782, when they were remade to a design of Sabatini with benches made of Colmenar stone, marble columns (originally carved for the great hall of the Casa de Legamarejo and reused here), and a top in the form of a quarter sphere with pediment and Cupid figurines made of

"The royal seat of Aranjuez ... is admirably situated at the confluence of the rivers Tagus and Jarama, which run through the gardens and add further charms to this delightful spot, where art and nature seem to go hand in hand in the most rustic and simple manner [...] the union and concentration at one point of all these things, fills the imagination with pleasing ideas, and impresses the traveller's mind with a thousand agreeable sensations, especially in springtime, when everything is in full bloom, and leads him to look upon Aranjuez as one of the most beautiful place in Europe."
John TALBOT DILLON: *Travels through Spain...*,London, 1780.

The Bacchus Fountain as originally conceived by Giambologna, with the Samson sculpture. Uffizi Gallery, Florence.

Cybele, bronze sculpture by Algardi in the Neptune fountain, Island Garden.

lead, as seen in the drawing by A. López Aguado and in the painting by Brambilla. One of these four upper sections was ruined in 1867, and instead of remaking it the decision was taken to eliminate the other three. The *Harpies Fountain* was built in 1615-17 by Juan Fernández and Pedro de Garay, both of Toledo; in the centre is a reproduction of the Boy with the Thorn, after the cast of the classical figure brought back from Italy by Velázquez. It was probably not placed here until 1660 or 1669 (when we have documentation of the fountain being repaired), but Madame d'Aulnoy refers to it in its present position in 1679.

The *Venus Fountain* has also, since the sixteenth century, been known as the "Don John of Austria Fountain", because legend has it that the stone of the upper bowl is from the Gulf of Lepanto. The fountain was sent from Florence to Aranjuez in 1571 by García de Toledo. Its style is close to that of the Florentine Mannerist sculptor, Giambologna, who made a similar fountain for the Villa Petraia with the same motif of Venus rinsing her hair, from which water springs out, as she steps from the bath. This fountain has lost "four boys made of white marble, with birds in their hands", which used to be on the edge of the lower basin, as shown in seventeenth-century engravings.

In the Bacchus fountain, the sculpture by Jonghellink which gives the ensemble its name is not the most outstanding feature: more important is the base made of Tuscan marble from Serravezza, carved by Giambologna (1566-1570), the original design of which is in the Uffizi Gallery. This fountain arrived in Spain in 1602 as a gift from the Grand Duke of Tuscany to the Duke of Lerma; it later passed to Philip III, who had it placed in the orchard of La Ribera in Valladolid. In 1623, Philip IV gave the sculptural group (by Giambologna) of *Samson and the Philistine*, which originally surmounted it, to Charles I of England; this is now in the Victoria and Albert Museum, London. In 1661 the same King ordered the Florentine base to be placed here, surmounting it with a Flemish sculpture, companion to others which are in the Hall of Columns in Madrid's Royal Palace.

The bronze sculptures decorating the *Neptune Fountain* were originally intended for the old palace in Madrid. During the second journey of Diego Velázquez to Rome, he personally commissioned them from the sculptor Alessandro Algardi as fireplace andirons for the palace's octagonal hall, but they were finally sent to the Aranjuez garden in 1661. There were four groups, and they represented the elements personified in Juno, Jupiter, Neptune and Cybele; two copies were made of each. Seven were placed on the fountain, and the eighth, Jupiter, was sent to the Buen Retiro. During the 19th century one of the lower groups with its pedestal was eliminated; and after the Civil War the other group of Jupiter and one of Juno disappeared. In 1751 Bonavia proposed that the fountain be redesigned, which was only carried out in part. It is currently under restoration.

The water for all the fountains came from the deposit called the "Sea of Ontígola", brought through lead pipes which were substituted by iron ones during the period of Philip V. The curious brick obelisk in the second third of the garden, towards the inlet, is one of the lead pipeline's "airholes"; the other, visible in one of the paintings by Houasse, was in the present Plaza de San Antonio, being demolished by Bonavia when he layed out this space. Water for the garden was also taken from the River Tagus, and filtered by the "clearwater machine" that was removed by Bachelieu to leave room for the Parterre.

The Neptune fountain in the Island Garden. Sculptures by Algardi.

The Prince's Garden in its beginnings:

The first or "Spanish" garden, between Calle del Embarcadero and the river from the round plaza, had three groves of trees (locust trees, elms and western planes) between which there were "small meadows or lawns with little trees; some spaces have flowers and rose bushes that cut to the same size produce a marvellous effect in the rose season," in accordance with English taste.

The *second garden*, to the right of Calle del Embarcadero, was in reality an orchard for "exquisite fruit trees and some vegetables; in it there is a square exclusively for the cultivation of carnations; it has more than a hundred and forty between orange, lemon and apple trees..." Between this orchard and the Tagus there were two strips of garden: "one contains a thicket of black poplars growing close together, planted in staggered parallel rows; the other presents the English idea of nature, without any sort of contrivance: it is longer than it is wide; its paths are uneven and twisting, and the weeping willows, myrtles, maples, cedars and laurels form an artificial vault, carpeted by soft herbs winding over sandy rides. This latter section, which Boutelou called "the wilderness," is occupied today by the Royal Barge Museum.

In addition to those described above, there were other fountains in the Island Garden, mentioned by 17th and 18th-century travellers but which later disappeared (such as the Fountain of Ganymede or Diana), or were transferred to other royal residences (such as the Fountain of the Tritons, which has been in the park of the Royal Palace in Madrid since 1846).

The latter appears to be Italian work of the late 16th century, but no information exists regarding its arrival; the first news we have is an order of Philip V in 1656 to place it at what was then the end of the island, in a small plaza enclosed by a wall, beyond which an avenue linked the bridges over the inlet and the Tagus, communicating the Calle de Madrid with the Picotajo orchards. The island ended downstream in a spit of land which the sediment deposited by the River Tagus gradually enlarged. In 1729, Philip V decided to make an ornamental garden or parterre there, on strong retaining walls, as a mirador or vantage-point over the River Tagus; he demolished the wall that had formed the boundary of the island, so bringing the path to the Picotajo into the garden. This appendage of the already centuries-old garden was called the *Islet*; it was built between 1731 and 1737 by Leandro Bachelieu, following the project drawn up by Etienne Marchand. It contained seven ponds, in one of which the Fountain of the Tritons was reconstructed. The stout walls were later rebuilt by Bonavia, who was also the architect of the new bridges over the inlet and the River Tagus, built in 1748 for the exclusive use of the Monarchs. The gateways were made more luxurious than originally planned, in 1750, "due to the frequent use made of them by the Queen," following a design by Ventura Rodríguez. The only gateway still existing today is the one giving onto the stone bridge spanning the inlet, completed in 1751. The other was built four years later and removed in 1869 with the intention of installing it in the Plaza de las Parejas, which did not occur. The wooden bridge leading from the Islet to the Picotajo was rebuilt twice, and disappeared definitively due to flooding by the river in the 19th century.

If we return towards the Palace by way of the terrace on the inlet, the present railing of which replaced the former stone parapet in 1845, we come to the *middle bridge*, a simple construction by Marquet dating from the reign of Charles III. Almost at the end are the stone steps and pedestals of the Chinese gazebo, a wooden structure that collapsed in the 19th century. It was built by Giacomo Bonavia in 1755-1757 on the inlet wall, so as to offer a view over the plaza in front of the Palace.

The 18th century contributed a new element to the garden, which travellers at the end of that century considered the island's greatest charm: neglect. The freedom with which the trees had been allowed to grow gave the impression that it was a "natural" garden, forgetting the character of the Renaissance scheme, the main elements of which (fountains, pavilions, galleries of greenery) had all fallen into decay or disappeared entirely. With

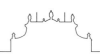

The first gateway, Puerta del Embarcadero, entering the Prince's Garden.

Farinelli, the famous castrato Carlo Broschi, protagonised and directed the operas and serenatas for Ferdinand VI and Barbara de Braganza, both of whom were great lovers of music. This musical entertainment found its most ingenious and elaborate scenario on the waters of the river, in the brillant series of late Baroque gondolas called the "River Tagus squadron" or "fleet", which navigated up-river from the Palace dam, to the hunting coverts in the grove. It was necessary to build a dockyard to store these barges, and a landing-stage was added to facilitate the King's access to the boats. The place selected for this was the end of the spit of land formed by the first bend in the river; besides its natural advantages, the site was well integrated into the Residence's urban plan: a straight avenue, perpendicular to Calle de la Reina, that started from the same place as the latter. The landing-stage, royal pavilion and avenue were finished in 1754.

the restoration projects initiated some ten years ago, a start has been made at recovering the original splendour of the island.

The Prince's Garden, the Royal Barge Museum and the Real Casa del Labrador

Of the avenues radiating from the front of the Parterre, the one closest to the River Tagus is *Calle de la Reina*, which is by far the oldest feature of the whole area as it was designed in its entirety by Juan Bautista de Toledo during the reign of Philip II. To the left (between the avenue and the river) the Monarch had orchards and gardens planted, and these were later extended by Ferdinand VI; the remainder of the land, adjoining the river, was a grove of trees until a great landscape garden was created on the entire site at the end of the 18th century.

The Prince's Garden

This garden was begun by Carlos IV when he was still Prince of Asturias, and finished while he was King between 1789 and 1808. In contrast to the Island Garden, this is a landscape garden following late 18th-century English and French fashion. However, it must not be forgotten that the scheme included earlier elements, such as the Spring Orchard and the landing-stage of Ferdinand VI, and that what Charles IV created here was not one garden but several.

It is entered through the first of the monumental gateways, *Puerta del Embarcadero*. Continuing along the *Calle del Embarcadero*, to the

Gondola used by Charles II on the Retiro lake and by Philip V at La Granja. Royal Barge Museum.

The Apollo Fountain.

The Prince's Garden on the Aranjuez Map by Santiago Loup, 1811. National Geographic Institute.

right lies the old *Spring Orchard* and to the left the River Tagus, which describes a curve seen at the end of this avenue: the landing-stage gives its name to the avenue and is preceded by a square with five picturesque pavilions. The largest is the royal pavilion, built by Bonavia in 1754, while the other four were constructed during the reign of Charles III for the enjoyment and recreation of the Prince and Princess of Asturias, Charles and María Luisa. At the same time a small octagonal garden was laid out to serve as a courtyard of honour separating Calle del Embarcadero from the main pavilion. The Infante Gabriel had a similar recreation pavilion on the far side of the river.

These pavilions arranged around the landing-stage of Ferdinand VI were the basis of the preference the future Charles IV felt for this spot, where he would take walks on spring mornings, and hence for the Prince's Garden that grew by successive additions from 1772 onwards.

The project, or more precisely the series of extensions, are the work of the gardener Pablo Boutelou, who first organized a series of small landscape gardens in the fashion of the day in the residual spaces between the river and the other pre-existing features: the pavilions, Calle del Embarcadero, and the Spring Orchard. This was the inspiration behind the first five "gardens" or compartments, created between 1775 and 1784; the plan drawn up by Boutelou at that time allows us to imagine its original state, though its present appearance is now quite different due to the numerous subsequent modifications, some introduced by Charles IV himself.

Within the area of the first five gardens, there are two architectural features which are typical landscape-garden structures, both dating from the reign of Charles IV and intended to give a picturesque aspect to the green grove as viewed from the river; work on them was directed by the engineer Domingo de Aguirre. The first is the *Little Fort*, close to the landing-stage, which held a battery of small canons that fired salutes to the vessels as the Monarchs sailed along the Tagus. Further upstream, the *Castle* (never faced with Colmenar stone as originally planned, due to economic difficulties derived from the war with France) was used as a mirador or vantage-point over the river, garden and groves of trees; its large vaulted halls, linked by stone spiral staircases, contain space reserved for a restaurant.

Facing the Castle is the *Royal Barge Museum*, built in 1963 according to a project of Ramón Andrada. Small boats and vessels used by Monarchs for excursions on the River Tagus are on display. These royal barges were formerly preserved in the old Casa de Marinos, built by Charles IV and restored by Amadeus of Savoy: part of this building still exists on the other side of the river.

The Prince's Garden in its beginnings: between the third and the fourth gardens were buildings dating from the period of Ferdinand VI, which were later demolished during the reign of Charles IV. The third, "Anglo-Chinese", garden "was planted to imitate the lovely disorder of nature and to conceal artifice, in the English manner, as seen in the mixture of various types of trees, planted in groups, which line the twisting paths, and in the new elements that present themselves to view as one strolls along them…" The fourth garden may have undergone some changes in respect of the original project while it was being planted, converting the straight avenues into curved ones, but the central oval space remained the same. "…it is like a big meadow, traversed by twisting paths going in different directions: the three widest ones lead to an oval plaza, being twenty-five feet in diameter. The width of the avenues varies, but all are adorned with many classes of trees, both American and other. The meadows are adorned with flowers, arranged in groups or by themselves, with rosebushes, myrtles, arbutus, lilacs, rubber and mangrove trees…"

The Boutelou family formed a long and complex dynasty of gardeners, very important for the Royal Residences during the 18th century. Esteban (I) was hired by Philip V around 1716, when he was already working in Aranjuez; later he played an important role in La Granja, where he died in 1735. His son Esteban (II), Head Gardener of Aranjuez during the reigns of Ferdinand VI and Charles III and part of that of Charles IV, was the most outstanding personality of the family, and it could be said that in good measure the splendour of the vegetation in Aranjuez is due to him. But the most accomplished professional of this saga was his son, Pablo, who was sent to France in 1764 to study with the gardeners of the Most Christian King. He then visited England and Holland, where he assimilated the landscape style. Other members of this family, including Fernando, Claudio and two more called Esteban, continued to run the royal gardens in the 19th century.

None of the vessels of Farinelli's delirious "Tagus Squadron" are preserved; nevertheless, one item in the Museum is equally Baroque and spectacular, and is even older: the so-called "gondola of Philip V," which in fact dates from the reign of Charles II (before 1668). It was probably built in Naples. During the 17th century it sailed on the lake of the Buen Retiro in Madrid, but in 1725 Luis I had it sent to La Granja so that Philip V, then in retirement there, could make use of it. Subsequently, it was stored at La Granja until being installed in this museum. The rest of the royal flotilla preserved here is from Aranjuez itself. The most outstanding vessels are those of Charles IV, Ferdinand VII, and the barge given to Isabel II by the city of Mahón.

Returning to the garden, we go through the area between the old Spring Orchard and the river. The *Narcissus Fountain* was built in the time of Charles IV, but due to damage during the French occupation, it was rebuilt in 1827 by Joaquín Dumandre who was inspired in the Fountain of the Satires that decorated the main parterre of the Villa Albani in Rome, well known from 1761 onwards. Around this fountain was situated the "third garden". The centre of the "fourth garden" was occupied by an oval plaza where, before 1804, the *Ceres Fountain* was installed, also destroyed and rebuilt in 1828; now only the base remains, because the sculptural group was transferred to the Parterre at the beginning of the 20th century.

The *Calle de Apolo* (or de Isabel II) is now reached. During the reign of Charles III the five sectors then making up the Prince's Garden ended here, bounded on this side by a ditch or ha-ha, replaced under Charles IV by the present avenue.

The *Apollo Fountain*, which closes the perspective of this avenue in a scenographic manner, is the only fountain of an architectural character in the Prince's Garden, since the others were purely sculptural, though it should be remembered that the original scheme of Charles IV had to be cut back for economic reasons. In 1789-90 the intention was to place this statue on the rock with the spring of the Chinese pond, but soon afterwards this idea was discarded and the present site was selected. The fountain was begun in 1803, but was not finished until the reign of Ferdinand VII, in accordance with a "new invention and design" by Isidro González Velázquez towards 1828.

The Apollo sculpture, "an old and very good piece" according to Quindós, is not from the period of Charles IV; it was formerly in the Palace of La Granja de San Ildefonso, being transferred to Aranjuez at the end of 1789. At La Granja it was in the central room on the ground floor, where Ponz saw it in 1787, attributing it to the hand of Fremin or Thierry, but possibly it is a 17th-century work from France or Italy.

Work on the gardens on the other side of this avenue was not begun until 1785, and so they do not appear in Boutelou's plan, which dates from the previous year. This sixth section of the garden was called

Detail of an embroidered tapestry in the Queen's Chamber, Real Casa del Labrador, with the pond and Chinese pagoda of the Prince's Garden in their original state. Real Casa del Labrador.

"Anglo-Chinese", and the most notable elements are found around the *Chinese pond*. Boutelou could work here on a large scale without any spatial or functional limitations obliging him to reduce his scope, and he also had available a greater wealth of materials and sculptures. It is not clear whether the landscaping is by Boutelou or Villanueva, but the latter is undoubtedly responsible for the architectural features decorating this area.

The Chinese *gazebo* built by Villanueva (the appearance of which is preserved in an embroidered hanging in the Casa del Labrador), disappeared as a result of the French invasion. The present gazebo dates from the time of Ferdinand VII, and is by the hand of González Velázquez, who followed the same groundplan but introduced considerable changes in its elevation. It has recently been repainted in its original colours, just as it appears in the painting by Brambilla. However, the circular temple with Ionic columns is the original one built by Villanueva, who had to incorporate the ten green Italian marble columns brought from La Granja, where Philip V had sent them. Also from this Monarch's collection were the Egyptian idols once placed on pedestals between the columns; these had been bought from the heirs of Queen Christina of Sweden, and are now in the Prado Museum.

The architectural decoration of the pond is completed by two artificial rock formations: the first, from which flowed the water to fill the pond, was intended to be surmounted by a statue of Apollo, but this was finally placed on the Apollo Fountain; the second rock formation was the base of an obelisk, the stone for which was selected for its similarity to oriental hazelnut granite, in accordance with Villanueva's

The Prince's Garden in its beginnings: the sixth garden "...His Highness ordered that the trees there when it was still a grove should be preserved, that was in the year 1785; there are white poplars, oaks and thorn ashes...He had artificial meadows made and the avenues lined with Lombardy poplars and plane trees. There are trees of many kinds in the meadows, such as cypresses from the Levant and our own, cedars of Lebanon and red cedars from Virginia, pines, Judas trees and many more. At the foot of the large trees, vines have been planted to intertwine and link them together: Greek Periploca, Carolina Pasaloides which produce bunches of blueish grapes, Virginia creeper, Virginia jasmine; all types of climbing plants that intertwine and grow up to the tops of the highest trees, some of which are being decorated with ivy, so that in a short time this garden will be the most capricious and varied that anyone could imagine. Other classes of creeping plants, such as the honeysuckle and passion flower, which climb less than the others, have been planted to grow on the small and medium-sized trees..." ALVAREZ DE QUINDOS, 1804.

Painting by Fernando Brambilla showing the Chinese pond. Patrimonio Nacional.

Vista del estanque llamado de los peces, en el jardín del Príncipe.

The seventh garden "was later expanded with many variations from the others" around 1794. Charles III ordered the construction of a sinuous estuary with several islands, as an allegory of the confluence of the Tagus and the Jarama: a statue on this theme used to preside the fountain from which the waters of this inlet played. This fountain was the work of Joaquín Arali, and it was finished in 1796. On a nearby isle was the Casa del Ermitaño (hermit's house); a rustic pavilion on the outside but very rich within. "The King, the Queen and the favourite are attacked by the mania for what they fancy to be improvement, and they are levelling ground, smoothing banks and raising artificial rocks with pagodas and Chinoiseries. The trees ... which I so admired seven years ago for their natural beauty and strength, are beginning to be trimmed and tortured into what the gardeners call lovely shapes... Nothing pleases the well-intentioned Monarch so much as the fiction of descending to the life of the lower classes and escaping the attentions of his Court, his Council and his people, and so he hardly sets foot in Madrid, and in all the corners of the royal gardens and parks capricious buildings are rising up."
William BECKFORD: *Italy, with Sketches of Spain and Portugal...*[1795], London 1834.

design. It was all built around 1791. A "Chinese-style boat", in the manner of a small gondola, was also built to navigate the pond.

This sixth garden ends in the *Calle de las Islas Americanas y Asiáticas* (or de Carlos III), where the seventh garden starts, and extends to the *Calle del Blanco* (or de Francisco de Asís), being divided into two parts by the *Calle del Malecón*. The notable landscaping of this part of the garden, begun in 1793, is now very disfigured.

Work on the section between the sixth and seventh gardens and the river was initiated in the same period. In the 19th century it was known as the zone of the American and Asiatic Isles, due to the exotic origin of the vegetation, arranged beside winding paths, on hills and along artifical streams. Most of the exotic species of plants brought in by Charles IV, and mentioned in 18th-century descriptions, must have been concentrated in this area, where botanical richness rather than design constitutes the most valuable element. It appears that in this most remote corner of the garden, Charles IV wished to have various architectural features built, such as the artificial mound known as the "montaña rusa", but these were never completed. Some interesting structures were begun at the base of the mound, with the appearance of a hall in basilica form, designed by Villanueva, but they were left unfinished. Later, during the reign of Ferdinand VII, his disciple Isidro González Velázquez limited himself to surmounting the work with a small square wooden temple, similar to the *gazebo* but much simpler.

The *eighth garden* begins in the old *Calle del Blanco*, known as *Calle de Francisco de Asís* since the reign of Alfonso XII when, in 1882, the traditional lines of Lombardy poplars were replaced by conifers. This garden surrounding the *Casa del Labrador* was created in 1803 after the

Lodge was finished, but it bears little resemblance to the original layout. At first, the *Casa del Labrador* was isolated by an old channel or river-bed of the Tagus, which was maintained as an inlet crossed by three wooden bridges. However, the inlet was eliminated by Isidro González Velázquez in 1828, and turned into a wide plaza with small trees and square flowerbeds which has gradually been reduced in size since that time.

The rest of the land between *Calle de la Reina* and the Tagus constitutes the *Miraflores Park*, created in 1848 by the Marqués de Miraflores, Palace Governor during the early years of the reign of Isabel II. It was designed by J. Whitby. This decayed park in the English style is not open to visitors.

THE REAL CASA DEL LABRADOR

This Royal Lodge, unlike the "cottages" built by Charles IV when he was still Prince, does not correspond to a coherent and preconceived architectural project; rather, it is the result of a building process lasting over ten years. The refinement of its design does not correspond to the flimsiness of the foundations and materials, or to the careless manner in which the new parts were built, without matching them well with the pre-existing sections. The head architect Juan de Villanueva, his helpers Antonio López Aguado and particularly Isidro González Velázquez, and the French decorator J.D.Dugourc, all collaborated in its creation. It is difficult to decide to what extent the second phase of construction was the responsibility of Velázquez alone or whether the head architect was involved, and also whether Villaneuva had any part in the interior decoration.

Construction of the Lodge was begun before 1791, and it was finished in 1803, with two clearly-differentiated phases being evident. The first, with Villanueva as the undisputed author, consisted of erecting a building based on a rectangular floor plan (the present central section, with a lower main floor and attic), without external decoration and faced in brick and rectangles of unplastered rough stone. This is how it appears in the two views of the Lodge "as it was in 1798," painted by Isidro González Velázquez. The second phase was carried out between 1799 and 1800, being completed in 1803 with a general remodelling of all the exteriors; it involved the construction of two wings enclosing a courtyard of honour, having two porticos with lowered arches in granite and terraces above. By way of the right-hand portico, coaches could go out to the other side of the Lodge, crossing a hallway next to the servants' staircase.

In this second phase of construction, all the architectural elements can clearly be attributed to Villanueva; not so the interior decoration, where, as we shall see, an important role was played by Dugourc. Lastly, the finishing touches were given during the third phase of construction,

Juan de Villanueva (1739-1811) is the major architect of Spanish Neoclassicism. He received his formation in the construction of the new Royal Palace in Madrid, and in the recently-created San Fernando Academy of Fine Arts, with his brother Diego, who was also an architect and the spreader of Neoclassical ideas in Spain. In 1758 Juan won a scholarship to study in Rome, which profoundly influened his style. After his return from Italy in 1765, he was appointed Architect of the Royal Monastery of San Lorenzo de El Escorial, of the Infantes and of the Prince (the future Charles IV), who appointed him Head Architect in 1797 on the death of Sabatini. Some of his principal works are in Madrid, including the Prado Museum, the Botanical Garden and the Astronomical Observatory; others are at El Escorial. In Aranjuez, where his activity was very intensive during the reign of Charles IV, his Classical style materialized above all in the small Ionic temple beside the *Chinese pond*, and in the gateway to Calle de la Reina, both in the Prince's Garden. However, in general the works he would undertake here were very different from his grandiose Classical style, by reason of both the materials (particularly in the *Casa del Labrador*) and the design, since he had to assimilate English and other exotic influences for the garden and its constructions, especially the Chinese temple, as well as in his intervention in planning the garden layout together with the Gardener, Pablo Boutelou. His disciple and follower, **Isidro González Velázquez**, developed Villanueva's less decisive traits into the ornamental style visible in the exterior decoration of the Casa del Labrador.

Isidro González Velázquez. Façade of the Real Casa del Labrador. Biblioteca Nacional.

View of the main staircase of the Real Casa del Labrador from the second floor.

consisting of the remodelling of the entire exterior with rich architectural decoration in plaster applied to the smooth brick and rough stone façade. The decorative spirit of this new exterior, including the fragility of the materials, distances this work from Villanueva's style and is closer to that of Isidro González Velázquez, who was named Assistant Head Architect of the Royal Palaces and Country Seats the following year. The interior decoration is preserved intact, but the deficient structure of the building and flimsiness of the external decoration have required two profound restorations, one in 1903 when the foundations were reinforced, and another in 1964-68, by Ramón Andrada, who replaced the roof frame by a metal structure.

In the *Courtyard of Honour*, where the cut-stone porticos were being carved to Villanueva's designs in July 1800, we can observe all the somewhat precious decoration of the exterior, which was finished in 1803 as witnessed by an inscription on the façade: bossed stone in horizonal bands on the ground floor, vaulted niches with sculptures and canopies over the balconies on the main floor, and flower garlands with "putti" on the attic level. However, the surfaces we now see are not the original ones, since the plaster was badly maintained and reached the 20th century in a poor state of repair. They were refaced with composition stone by R. Martín Gamo during the 1964-68 restoration.

The **ground-floor rooms** were painted by Japelli during the reign of Charles IV, but flooding by the Tagus in the late 19th and early 20th centuries caused these decorations to be lost, and the present aspect

Main staircase, Real Casa del Labrador.

dates from Andrada's restoration. However, the rooms on the main floor preserve the decoration of Charles IV in all their splendour and luxury; all the items belong to the same period, unless the contrary is indicated. The magnificent silk draperies are, in their majority, from Lyons, but there are also Valencian silk hangings, made by the Bodoy family. The Royal Factory wove rich carpets for the Lodge, with "Pompeian" motifs designed by Manuel Pérez, but they are now kept at the Royal Palace in Madrid.

The vestibule contains an eighteenth-century plaster copy of the *Castor and Pollux*, which used to be in the Palace of La Granja de San Ildefonso, and two busts of *Mars* and *Minerva* from the same palace, both Roman works of the 17th century.

The Main Staircase, built in 1799, is rich in marbles, bronzes and mahogany. Villanueva must have followed designs of Dugourc, who in turn was inspired by the staircase created in 1787 by Brogniart for the Parisian palace of the Prince of Massserano, Ambassador of Charles IV. The charm of the movement suggested by the two semicircular flights is enjoyed upon arriving at the main landing, with sculptures by Hermenegildo Silici. Outstanding is the relief with portraits of Charles and María Luisa over the entrance door leading to the rooms. The two busts of *Juno* and *An Amazon* also came from La Granja.

From here it is possible to out onto one of the terraces overlooking the courtyard, decorated with 17th and 18th-century Italian busts based on classical models.

Jean-Demosthène Dugourc, French decorator and architect, was mainly responsible for introducing the ornamental repertory fashionable during the reign of Charles IV, for whom he designed furniture, bronzes and silks (woven by the prestigious Pernon firm of Lyons), not only during his stay in France but also in Spain, where Dugourc settled in 1800 and remained until the Napoleonic invasion. His original and imaginative style is easily recognizable, although written references to his activities are more difficult to find. As a result, it is no simple matter to discern his role in some of the rooms where we know work was supervised either by Villanueva (the Hall of Mirrors in the Palace) or by Isidro González Velázquez (the "water-closet" in the Casa del Labrador), since it seems that the architects limited themselves to supervising the execution of the work designed by the interior-decoration specialist.

Billiard Room, Real Casa del Labrador.

The **King's Room**, or **Billiard Room**, with a table already suggesting the style of Ferdinand VII, has a ceiling painted in 1799 with frescoes by Maella, representing *The Four Elements*. Notable is the splendid and fascinating wall-hanging woven in Lyons with views of Madrid and the Royal Residences, in decorative frames inspired in the Vatican's *logge di Raffaello*, and characteristic of the subtle change from the "Etruscan" to "Empire" taste. The same is true of the fireplace, made of white marble with painted and gilt glass decoration. This was all designed by Dugourc. The big mahogany clock, of bronze, gilt carving and engraved crystal, is by Manuel de Rivas (1804). The frieze, beautifully painted in tempera, is by Manuel Muñóz de Ugena, as are those of all the other rooms.

The **Sculpture Gallery**, designed by Dugourc, is a brilliant example of the neoclassical taste; the complete articulation of its walls with the Corinthian order is achieved in plaster imitating marble to perfection.

The sculpted reliefs of the friezes and panels above the doors are by José Ginés. Charles IV commissioned some sculptures from Canova, but these never occupied their places in the niches on the long walls. The *busts of Greek philosophers and writers* were from the collection of José Nicolás de Azara, Ambassador in Rome and a friend of Mengs, bequeathed by Azara to Charles IV. Almost all are from the Villa Adriana in Tivoli, and most are Roman copies of Greek originals. They were placed in the gallery during the reign of Ferdinand VII, and somewhat overload the original decoration and spaciousness of the room, as does the colossal *Trajan's Column Clock*, a French piece bought by Charles IV from Godon's widow in 1803. The ceiling paintings are by Zacarías González Velázquez, being dated between 1800 and 1806. They portray Night, Day, the Morning Star, the Milky Way, allegories of Agriculture, the Arts and Industry, and at the ends, Flora and Bacchus.

Sculpture Gallery, Real Casa del Labrador.

Sculpture Gallery, Real Casa del Labrador: detail of the Trajan's Column clock.

Detail of the Lyons silk wall-hangings in the Ballroom, Real Casa del Labrador.

Dugourc, who was collaborator and brother-in-law of the architect Bélanger, was one of the principal designers in the transition from the Louis XVI style to the Empire style, as he extended the sources of classical inspiration of the former with a highly varied range of exotic and historicist ornamental repertoires, especially the Egyptian and "Etruscan", or in other words the Greek art known due to the recent archaeological discoveries in Italy.

The floor of this room contains a rich combination of Spanish marbles, and was made by the marble workers from the Palace Workshop, under the direction of Renzo Poggetti; but in this case it is further enriched by six fragments of Roman mosaic from Mérida.

The **Queen's Lobby** is decorated with rich silk drapery made in 1803 by the King's Court-embroiderer, Juan López de Robredo, with oval cameos, birds, frets, garlands and other motifs from the Herculanean repertory, on a cream-coloured background. The ceiling, with *Orpheus and Eurydice* among Pompeian decorations, is by Manuel Pérez.

The **Terrace Sitting Room** can only be glimpsed from the door: the Valencian drapery is plain silk painted with flowers; the ceiling, by Juan Duque, represents *Agriculture*. The tabletop, from the end of the 18th century, contains a selection of marbles that do not appear to be Spanish.

The **Corner Room**, with wall-hangings of Lyons silk by Pernon, socle of painted butterflies, and ceiling by Juan Duque with oriental birds and the arms of Spain, is furnished with a set of console tables and corner cabinets, on which stand French clocks and vases from the first third of the 19th century.

Queen Maria Luisa's Room, Real Casa del Labrador: the painted ceiling is by Maella and the Lyons wall-hangings by Pernon.

A corner of the Ballroom, Real Casa del Labrador.

Detail of the Ballroom fireplace, Real Casa del Labrador.

Detail of a ceiling in the east wing of the Real Casa del Labrador.

Room of the Christ, Real Casa del Labrador.

Anteroom. Zacarías González Velázquez painted the ceiling, which is in three compartments, portraying *Apollo and the Muses*, the rape of *Ganymede* and the rape of *Helen*. Wall-hangings from *Lyons* by Pernon. The clocks and vases are French, from the first third of the 19th century.

Queen María Luisa's Room. The ceiling fresco is by Maella (1798), and represents *Peace and her Benefits on Human Work in each of the Four Seasons*. The frieze has painted landscapes in medallions and circular mouldings on canvas. The luxurious *tapestry* woven in Lyons by Pernon after designs by Dugourc, like that of the Billiard Room, has ninety-three views of Aranjuez, El Escorial and various other places in Spain and Italy; particularly interesting, with regard to Aranjuez, are the two views of the pond in the Prince's Garden, with the small Chinese temple by Villanueva before its destruction during the Napoleonic invasion. The four panels over the doors and window are larger compositions, also animated by the taste for classical antiquity. Above the mantelpiece of Carrara marble, the Ceres clock is an important work by Godon, Court-clockmaker to Charles IV; the others are from the first third of the nineteenth century. The floor, from the first period of the Lodge's construction, is made of porcelain. The three console tables and twelve chairs, designed by Dugourc, are the original furniture.

Principal Room or Ballroom. This is the most spacious room in the Lodge, and its floor is of parquet, not marble. The painted ceiling was begun by Bayeu and finished by Maella, who signed it in 1792,

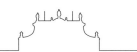

The Queen's Lobby, Real Casa del Labrador.

Marble and mosaic floor in the Water Closet, Real Casa del Labrador.

representing *The Power of the Spanish Monarchy in the Four Parts of the World*, with various allegories of Commerce, Agriculture, Industry, the Sciences and the Arts, around the figure of Spain. The furniture, with rich console tables and chairs decorated with lions, dates from the reign of Ferdinand VII, except for the monumental *clock* with organ music and kettledrums, made between 1798 and 1804 after designs by

A corner of the Platinum Room, Real Casa del Labrador.

Detail of the Water Closet stuccos, Real Casa del Labrador.

J.B. Ferroni, which is from the period of Charles IV, as is the rest of the sumptuous decorative programme. The silk wall-hangings woven in Lyons by Pernon, always after designs of Dugourc, in an "Etruscan red" colour with a yellow background, represent Pompeian motifs taken from the *Antiquities of Herculaneum* - women dancers, dancing satyrs, Jupiter and Janus - alternating so as to produce variety. The delicate inlaid marble *fireplace* displays the same motifs. The classical and naturalistic themes represented on the frieze painted on canvas are of great variety and delicacy. The large chandeliers of bronze and crystal,

The Corrine Room, Real Casa del Labrador.

like the clocks and vases, are French from the period of Ferdinand VII. The great Sèvres porcelain amphoras with painted landscapes are outstanding, being displayed on pedestals in the corners of the Room. The chair and table are made of Russian malachite in a pseudo-baroque style. They were wedding gifts of Czar Alexander III to Queen Isabel II in 1846, and break with the stylistic unity of the room.

The eastern wing of the Lodge has eight rooms, among them the two most precious ones. The clocks and porcelain purchased by Ferdinand VII are from Paris.

First Room. The ceiling was painted by Zacarías González Velázquez: *Neptune, Cupid, Venus and the Graces*, on canvas imitating woven tapestry. Part of the series of *Views of the Royal Residences* by Fernando Brambilla, portraying La Granja, Valsaín and Riofrío. The Lyons wall-hangings date from the period of Charles IV, and the furniture is in the style of Ferdinand VII.

Second Room. Ceiling with Pompeian-style paintings by Manuel Pérez.

Third Room. Ceiling with oil-painting by Manuel Pérez, of pastoral landscapes with Romantic ruins on the octogonal panels, framed by volutes and other Pompeian motifs inspired in the *logge*. These three rooms have Valencian draperies and furniture from the period of Charles IV.

Fourth Room. Ceiling decorated by Japelli with a variety of scenes: *Rape of the Sabine Women, Astronomers, Italian Peasants, Flight in a Balloon*, and *Lunardi's Descent by Parachute*. The decorative elements framing them are no less varied, since the majority are Pompeian, although a few have Gothic touches.

Fifth Room or **The Christ's Room**. The ceiling paintings are by Japelli with a variety themes of a Pre-Romantic and novelesque sensibility, framed with ornaments inspired in the ceilings of Rome's Domus Aurea. The pictures of the series Views of the *Royal Residences* by Brambilla, represent fountains and other aspects of La Granja. Drapery from Lyons by Pernon; furniture designed by Dugourc.

Platinum Room. This is the most luxurious and important room from an artistic viewpoint, since it is the work of Napoleon's architects and decorators, Percier and Fontaine, who later published it in their *Recueil de décorations intérieures*. The commission was given in 1802 and the work was mainly carried out in the period 1801-1807, not being completely finished until after 1808. The boiserie is of mahogany encrusted with gilt bronze and platinum, and the mirrors attempt to create the illusion that this small square space is a gallery, an effect particularly well-achieved in the arches of the semicircular ends of the room, where the mirrors reproduce the barrel vault. The Empire style shines forth here in all its purity and luxury. The paintings are worthy of their setting, as the large *Allegories of the Four Seasons* and the smaller *Allegories of Love, Science, and Music* in the circular mouldings are by Girodet. The four landscapes under the mirrors are by Bidaut; the views of the Louvre, Florence and Naples, by Chébeat.

The **Water Closet** is a masterpiece of the stucco-worker Antonio Marzal, imitating and even surpassing similar works of the Brilli brothers in Madrid's Royal Palace. It follows a model in which Isidro González Velázquez seems to follow the designs drawn by J.D.Dugourc. The Ionic pilasters frame panels decorated with such extreme refinement that the room results almost excessively precious.

"This (the Prince's) garden in Aranjuez without doubt constitutes one of the most pleasant promenades that exists in Europe; I owe it this praise in recompense for the delicious hours I spent in the shade of its foliage, wandering amongst its labyrinths of vegetation and flowers, amusing myself in the best possible way among the botanical riches of the old world and the new."
Jean-François BOURGOING: *Nouveau voyage en Espagne...*[1785], Paris 1788.

Perhaps the private nature of this room causes this difference in atmosphere compared to the Sculpture Gallery and the Staircase, both more sombre and monumental in their equally-reduced dimensions. The ceiling paintings are by Zacarías González Velázquez, and contain obvious allusions to *Air*, *Vigilance*, *Strength*, and *Repose*. The magnificent marble floor includes fragments of Roman mosaics. The console table with fasces and warriors, is really only the model of the table that was to have been made in bronze; the stools with gilt Egyptian heads are the originals.

The **Corrine Room** owes its name to the Greek poetess represented on the French clock in the centre of the room. The Pompeian ceiling is the best of those decorated here by Manuel Pérez. Paintings from the series of *Views of the Royal Residences* by Brambilla, portray fountains and other aspects of La Granja. Furniture of Charles IV.

The **Last Room** has a ceiling painted by Juan Duque, inspired in the paintings of Rome's Domus Aurea; further pictures of the same series by Brambilla; the frieze, as in the previous room, is stucco-work, and the drapery from Lyons by Pernon. The tour continues by re-entering the first room and Ballroom.

Entrance to the Water Closet from the Platinum Room, Real Casa del Labrador.

The Water Closet, Real Casa del Labrador.

Gateway into the Prince's Garden leading to the Casa del Labrador.

The **Royal Stud Room**, has canvases by Zacarías González Velázquez covering the ceiling and walls, with a similar feeling of *horror vacui* that led to tapestries being hung in the winter palaces of El Pardo and El Escorial. The paintings portray landscapes of Aranjuez, with Charles IV and Godoy hunting, horses from the Royal Stud (among them the extinct breed of horses with small "sheep-like" heads), and other countryside scenes. The furniture follows designs by Dugourc.

The **Servants' Staircase** is the original staircase of the Lodge. The charming trompe l'oeil mural paintings with figures in the fashions of the first decade of the 19th century, are by Zacarías González Velázquez.

The second floor has four small rooms which are not visited; the decoration dates from the reigns of Charles IV and Ferdinand VII, with ceilings by Juan Duque.

Town Planning in Aranjuez

From the Plaza de San Antonio it is worthwhile to walk along Calle de San Antonio, or along the "trident," for the planning of Aranjuez undertaken by Ferdinand VI was the most ambitious such project of the Spanish Court Baroque. Charles III also paid special attention to the planning of Aranjuez, due to the exemplary nature of this new model town of the Enlightenment Monarchy, which here tried to unite institutional pomp and splendour with the delights of country life. This interest was accentuated after the Mutiny of Esquilache (1766), which led to the Monarch's efforts for the urban renewal of Madrid to be extended towards the Royal Residence Towns. This period saw a start on the most ambitious buildings, an expansion of the town (1765), and the construction of facilities such as the cemetery and the slaughterhouse.

Aranjuez was the most regularly planned and arranged of the Royal Residence Towns, constituting the supreme example of the Spanish Enlightenment Court town, with an urban layout characteristic of the late international Baroque style, and magnificently functional buildings. In general, construction was governed by regularity, uniformity and decorum, with artistocratic palaces (such as those of Medinaceli, Osuna and Godoy) of three storeys and considerable size, and humbler dwellings of one or two storeys.

The tree-lined avenues lead visitors with an interest in urban planning beyond the town limits. The singularly interesting sixteenth-century layout is still maintained in the *Doce Calles* and Picotajo Orchards, on the far side of the river, but it should not be forgotten that both *Calle de Toledo* and *Calle de la Reina* are due to Philip II.

After a century and a half of maintenance without creation, Philip V, and above all Ferdinand VI, did not limit themselves merely to renovating the old schemes, but created new promenades such as the important Calle Larga (today without trees), leading from the *Long Bridge to Doce Calles*. However, in order to understand the great increase in the number and extension of the tree-lined avenues under Charles III, and the new image that Aranjuez then acquired, it is worthwhile to visit the *Cortijo de San Isidro*, continuing to the end of *Calle de la Reina*.

Scattered around the territory of the Royal Residence are notable buildings, destined for use by the model farms and practically all built under Charles III. Though they cannot be visited, it is worth mentioning the **Casa de Sotomayor** or **de la Monta**, built for the Royal Stud Farm by Marquet in 1761-1766; **Casa de Mira el Rey**, by Marquet, built for the employees of the Casa de Vacas, 1766; **Casa del Campo Flamenco**, 1775; **Casa de las Infantas**, from the reign of Ferdinand VII; **Casa de Villamejor**, for the breeding of mules, 1764, by Marquet; and **Real Cortijo de San Isidro**, the model farm most characteristic of the example of Enlightenment agriculture that Charles III wanted to give to Aranjuez, designed by Serrano, 1774-1782. **El Deleite** was also organized as a model farm in the period of Charles III, but the palace was built between 1852 and 1864 for the Queen Mother, María Cristina de Borbón, following a project by Alejandro Sureda.

BIBLIOGRAPHY

ALVAREZ DE QUINDOS Y BAENA, Juan Antonio: *Descripción histórica del real bosque y Casa de Aranjuez*, Madrid, 1804, Facsimile ed., Doce Calles, Aranjuez, 1993.

BONET CORREA, Antonio (Curator): *El Real Sitio de Aranjuez y el arte cortesano del siglo XVIII*, exhibition catalogue, Comunidad de Madrid, Palace of Aranjuez, April-May 1987. With bibliography by Yago Barja de Quiroga, and an interesting selection of eighteenth-century travellers' texts by Selina Blasco Castiñeyra.

BOTTINEAU, Yves: *L'Art de Cour dans l'Espagne de Philippe V.* Bordeaux, 1962. Spanish edition, Madrid, Fundación Universitaria Española, 1986.

BOTTINEAU, Yves: *L'Art de Cour dans l'Espagne des Lumières,* Paris, De Boccard, 1986.

CASA-VALDES, Marquesa de: *Jardines de España.* Madrid, Espasa-Calpe, 1973.

GROMORT, Georges: *Jardins d'Espagne.* Paris, 1926, vol. II.

IÑIGUEZ ALMECH, Francisco: *Casas reales y jardines de Felipe II.* CSIC, Roma, 1952, pp. 140-154.

JUNQUERA Y MATO, Juan José: *La decoración y el mobiliario en los Palacios de Carlos IV.* Madrid 1979, pp 121-143 and 152-160.

LOPEZ Y MALTA, Cándido: *Historia descriptiva del Real Sitio de Aranjuez. Sobre la que escribió en 1804 don Juan Alvarez de Quindós.* Aranjuez, 1869. Facsimile ed. Doce Calles, Aranjuez, 1988.

MADOZ, Pascual: *Diccionario histórico-estadístico de España y de sus posesiones de Ultramar.* Madrid, 1848, Vol.X, pp. 430-445.

MARTIN GONZALEZ, Juan José: "El Palacio de Aranjuez en el siglo XVI," Archivo Español de Arte, XXXV, núm. 139 (1962).

MOLEON GAVILANES, Pedro: *La arquitectura de Juan de Villanueva.* Madrid. COAM, 1988.

MORAN TURINA, Miguel, and CHECA CREMADES, Fernando: *Las Casas del Rey. Casas de campo, cazaderos y jardines. Siglos XVI y XVII.* Ed. El Viso, Madrid, 1986, esp. pp. 83-85, 93-98, 103-105, 134-139. *Ordenanzas para el gobierno del Real Sitio de Aranjuez.* Madrid, Imprenta Real, 1795, Facs. ed., Doce Calles, Aranjuez, 1990.

ORTIZ CORDOBA, Angel: *Aldea, Sitio, Pueblo. Aranjuez, 1750-1841,* Aranjuez, 1992.

PONZ, Antonio: *Viaje de España...,* Vol. I, Madrid, Ibarra, 1787, and additions in the 1793 edition, Vol. I, pp. 375-394.

REALES SITIOS. *Revista del Patrimonio Nacional* (since 1964). This magazine is mentioned generically, since the great number of articles about Aranjuez is too long to list.

RIVERA BLANCO, Javier: *Juan Bautista de Toledo y Felipe II: la implantación del clasicismo en España,* Universidad de Valladolid, 1984.

SANCHEZ MORENO, Pedro M.: "En torno a Aranjuez", a complete thematic bibliographic repertory on Aranjuez, in *Aranjuez y los libros,* exhib.cat., Sala Juan de Villanueva, Aranjuez, April 1987, pp. 21-42.

SANCHO, José Luis, y ATIENZA, Javier: "Cartografía histórica de Aranjuez. Cinco siglos de ordenación del territorio," Nº 3 of *Riada.* Studies on Aranjuez, Doce Calles, Aranjuez, 1991, 47 pp and 12 maps.

SANCHO, José Luis: *La Arquitectura de los Sitios Reales. Catálogo histórico de los palacios, jardines y patronatos reales del Patrimonio Nacional,* Patrimonio Nacional - Fundación Tabacalera, Madrid, 1995.

TARRAGA BALDO, María Luisa: "La fuente del Rey en la plaza principal de Aranjuez: Bonavía y Olivieri," A.E.A. num. 203 (1978), p. 287.

WINTHUYSEN, Xavier de: *Jardines clásicos de España. Castilla.* Madrid, 1930. Facsimile ed. with introductory study by Carmen Añón and notes by José Luis Sancho, Ed. Doce Calles, Madrid, 1989.

The printing of this book, published jointly by the Patrimonio Nacional and Aldeasa, was finished on the 2nd day of April, 1998, at Estudios Gráficos Europeos, Madrid

ROYAL PALACE

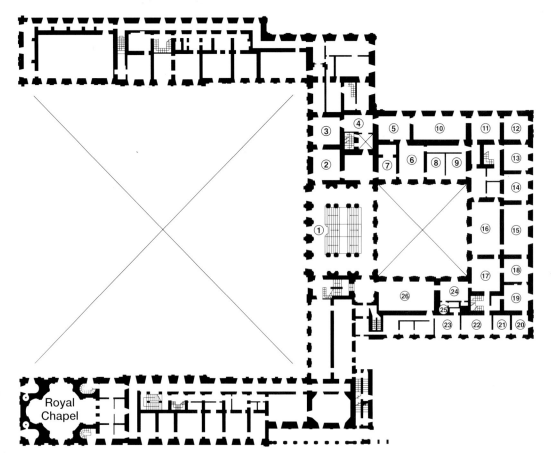

MAIN FLOOR

① Main Staircase
② Guard Room
③ Queen's Lobby
④ Queen's Antechamber
⑤ Queen's Chamber, or Queen's Music Room
⑥ Ante-Oratory
⑦ Oratory of Charles IV, later of Queen Isabel II
⑧ Isabelline Room
⑨ Children's Room
⑩ Throne Room
⑪ Queen's Study
⑫ Porcelain Room
⑬ Queen's Bedroom

⑭ Queen's Boudoir
⑮ Ballroom
⑯ Conversation Room
⑰ King's Chamber
⑱ King's Smoking Room, or Arab Room
⑲ Bedroom of King Francisco de Asís
⑳ Room of Queen María Luisa, or Hall of Mirrors
㉑ King's Study
㉒ King's Music Room
㉓ Gallery of Chinese Paintings
㉔ King's Antechamber
㉕ Oratory of Queen María Luisa
㉖ King's Guardroom